"People always ask, 'Why do 1 [the Reward], Randy Klassen un[the reader with a unique and rel_ _._ ,,uuun that goes far beyond himself to touch the broader, shared human desire for movement that we have lost in modernity. Throughout his stories, that venture beyond physical and mental boundaries, I identified with Randy's deep connection to community and was reminded that our greatest sources of power and inspiration come from feeling connected to one another through the shared struggle to survive life's hardships."

Jenny Quilty, 2019 Squamish50/50 Overall Winner and course record, 2022 UTMB Doi Inthanon 100-Mile Champion

"*Perhaps Joy is the Reward* will inspire those who desire to run for 100 miles or no miles at all. I met a new version of Randy when he pushed himself to go farther as he got older and to strive for finish lines that were unimaginable a decade before he turned sixty."

Steph Corker, 2016 Ironman Canada Champion and 26x Ironman finisher

"I met Randy when he was just starting out. Though much older than most new trail runners, he was determined to get stronger and set high expectations for himself. A decade later, Randy offers inspiration to Capra Trail Running Club members, especially the newbies who haven't quite grasped their potential ... yet."

Solana Green, Capra Running Co-Owner, 5 Peaks BC Race Director 2013–2021

PERHAPS JOY is the REWARD

A late start, going far,
and a 50/50 chance

Randy Klassen

THE
SELF
PUBLISHING
AGENCY

Randy Klassen
Perhaps Joy is the Reward

Copyright © 2023 by Randy Klassen
First Edition

Softcover ISBN 978-1-7380132-1-0
Hardcover ISBN 978-1-7380132-0-3
Electronic ISBN (Kindle) 978-1-7380132-2-7

Book Design | Petya Tsankova
Cover photo | Solana Green
Editor | Tara McGuire
Publishing Support | TSPA The Self Publishing Agency, Inc.

This book is for the Capra trail running community in Squamish, BC.

You care, cheer, and console. You make me better and stronger.

Most of all, this book is for Cindy, who encourages me to continue exploring and who fixes me when I come home broken.

A Note About Distances

In this book, I express distances in both miles and kilometres. In the ultrarunning world we can't do much about that with race distances of 50 kilometres, 50 miles, 100 kilometres, 100 miles, etc. I'm also a child of the 60s and had my world messed up on April Fools' 1975 when Canada switched from English standard units of measurement to metric. As a result, body weight is measured in pounds, butter is purchased in kilograms, my height is in feet and inches, temperatures are in Celsius or Fahrenheit (I really don't care which), and I wonder what kind of mileage my Jeep will get on a litre of fuel when we 4x4 up to an elevation 1,000 metres to begin our hike to the summit of a 7,260-foot mountain. I interchange English standard and metric in this book because I'm Canadian and I can't run away from that. Sorry.

For readers who weigh themselves in pounds or kilograms:
- 1 mile is 1.6 kilometres
- 1 kilometre is 0.62 miles
- A 10K is about 6 miles
- For 20 kilometres, think half-marathon distance
- For longer distances, comparisons will appear where I feel they might be helpful

Contents

Prologue

On August 19, 2017, six weeks past my fifty-fifth birthday, and 12 kilometres into the arduous Squamish50-Mile ultramarathon, DeBeck's Hill loomed before me.

The ice-age rubble pile of DeBeck's was the first taxing obstacle that stood between me and the successful finish of my first 50-mile (82-kilometre) ultra. The sky above DeBeck's had a faint orange tinge, the smoky remnants of a heavy forest fire season in BC. But the airborne particulate count was safe, the air was cool, and the humidity low—perfect trail racing conditions.

I'd paced myself well from the start, and then, as I crossed the narrow bouncing bridge of rough split logs over Hop Ranch Creek to tackle the 400-metre vertical slug up DeBeck's, my breath quickened and my shoulders and upper arms tightened—the exact opposite of how I needed to relax into the uphill. In the still, moss-blanketed forest that clung to DeBeck's slopes, my mind muttered nonsensical questions about my training and preparedness. Would this first climb zap my strength and leave me wanting on the biggest climb of the day, the aptly named Galactic Schiesse, a half-marathon distance beyond DeBeck's? And if I struggled on the Galactic climb, would I then have nothing left for all the pesky climbs in the last 28 kilometres of the race—the section of continuous ups and downs that all added up to make the end of the run harder than its beginning?

I started the laborious DeBeck's climb doubtful, not determined. In my mind, I'd been giving that mountain the power to beat me throughout the weeks I'd been envisioning my race.

And then I met a girl.

No, this isn't *that* kind of story. I met a girl wearing a racing bib, a fellow runner. I fell in step behind her, and together we shared the suffering of raising high knees higher, and reaching for roots to pull ourselves up the inclines, and slipping together on the loose grit on the granite. I've never had the capacity to remember temporary trail-buddy names, and that case was no different, so I will call her Ann.

Tall and fit, in her late twenties or maybe early thirties (I've always been atrocious with guessing ages, too), Ann told me her story as we climbed.

Ann was on a revenge run.

One year ago, she was less than 10 kilometres from finishing her first Squamish50-Mile when, in her words, "They stole my race from me."

Slightly undertrained for the race's extreme vertical gain and loss (by her telling) and having barely escaped the strictly enforced time cutoff at the Far Side Aid Station, the final station before the finish, she arrived at a trail junction she called "that boardwalk place." There, to her utter dismay, she was pulled from the race by poorly informed course marshals who said it had been determined that she would be unable to reach the finish line in "reasonable enough time" after it closed for full race cutoff.

Almost seventeen hours of exertion and pain had been meted out on her in the mountains. Having braved those hardships nearly to the end, she was not allowed to slog out the hour or two it would take for her to get to the finish line. Above me on the hill, Ann firmly asserted, "I had the strength to make it to the end that night. But those course marshals just wouldn't let me. So, I got a DNF!" That loathsome "Did Not Finish" designation stamped behind a runner's name on the official race results when the runner *does not* cross the finish line.

Since that experience, Ann had trained tirelessly the whole

year to get back stronger and better able to conquer. I sensed purpose in her voice as she spoke about her improved fitness.

The tiresome vertical metres I had feared when I was down at the creek dissolved effortlessly under my feet as Ann unwound her year-old tale of defeat and how it felt to be back on the same trail now, more determined than ever to finish. As she spoke, I became oblivious to the state of my muscles as they carried me upwards through the dense forest and grey rock. My caustic inner voice ceased its negative nattering.

And guilt was growing inside me.

One year prior, on the night of Ann's DNF, my wife Cindy and I were the course marshals at "that boardwalk place" in the closing hours of the race. As the clock wound down to the seventeen-hour race cutoff time, Cindy's professional judgment as an ER nurse was called upon by the race-directing team to help determine which runners were capable of reaching the finish line in the designated time, and who needed to be escorted off the course at our location and driven to the finish.

Hard decisions were being made. Agonizing walkie-talkie debates were ongoing. Sweepers were being consulted about the pace of the lagging racers in the dark trees ahead of them. And then a runner—Ann—was being told her race was over. It had to be done. At the pace she was moving, she could not be supported to the end. The Squamish50 was a two-day race event. Day one needed to be wrapped up on schedule for the numerous volunteers, many of whom had to be up again after much too little sleep, to support hundreds of racers on Sunday. The back of the bus was a hard place to ride that night. Not everyone finished.

I was the guy who walked Ann off the course one year earlier in the black forest where our faces were unrecognizable blurs of shadow and glaring headlamps. I was the marshal she might have remembered as the knobby-kneed older man with a close-cut grey beard and potbelly. I was the one wearing the Australian cowboy

Outback hat, bashing that annoying tambourine to cheer runners and keep the bears at bay. I had literally, physically, taken 2016's race finish from the runner five feet ahead of me.

Climbing up DeBeck's, I confessed.

We climbed in silence for a while.

"It had to be done. I know that," Ann eventually said, her voice softer. Reflection replaced revenge. "But it was hard, you know. All that time spent, and then I failed, and I was so close." There was another lengthy pause. "But I know why you pulled me. I wasn't going to make cutoff."

More silent climbing.

"But I'm stronger now. I'm going to finish this race today."

Determination. Zero doubt. We kept talking, and I gained strength from her—and some forgiveness too. Most of all, what I gained from Ann's story was that she had willfully conquered her DNF demon from the year before and that the time had come for me, right there on that hill, to unseat the demon riding on my back—the one who gripped me tight when I crossed Hop Ranch Creek 2 kilometres earlier, the one who had been whispering in my ear that I was inadequate ever since I did not finish my Bryce Canyon 50K ultra two months earlier in an epic heatstroke collapse.

And then we emerged from the forested single track onto the peak of DeBeck's Hill. With a quick "goodbye" Ann ran away down the rocky forest service road the racecourse followed off the top of the mountain.

I stopped and took a selfie at the summit. Big smile. The first fearsome climb was done, and thanks to Ann, I felt stronger than when I started. The DeBeck's climb wasn't going to take my race from me. The self-doubt that fuelled my worries about the first big obstacle had been overcome in an inspiring conversation.

My body was trained and ready to climb that first difficult mountain and carry on strong—my mind was the problem.

Becoming engaged in Ann's comeback story reoriented my focus from my recent failure to striving for success.

From the top of DeBeck's onward, I never once doubted that I would finish my first 50-mile ultramarathon. I would gladly run every step of that race again; it was such a happy hard day. When I crossed the start line that morning, I was ready to do it; I just hadn't allowed myself to trust that readiness and fully believe in my training, my body, and myself.

I gained that belief from a fellow runner who was in the process of energetically and purposefully overcoming a full year of feeling defeated. I gained that belief through her story.

Ann finished well before me, and we hugged when I eventually got to the finish line scrum some fourteen hours after our DeBeck's encounter. No one can ever take that 2017 finish from her. She owned it like I owned my finish that day as well. There was great reward in that.

———

In the years that followed, I became the sweeper for the Saturday morning Capra Trail Running Club in Squamish, BC.

Now, my official job each week is to make sure no one in our pack of ten-to-twenty gets left behind as we weave through soaring Westcoast fir, spruce, and cedar, ascend rocky ridges, plummet down stone and root-littered descents, and that we regroup safely at every major intersection. My *actual* job is to keep the back-of-the-bus runners entertained for two-plus hours as we, the less fleet of foot, strive to keep up with our more energetic friends. And what better way to distract new, occasional, and recovering runners from the moment's hardships than with stories of my past ultra-racing miseries, hard-fought finishes, and lessons learned from thousands of kilometres of footfalls on mountain dirt. And if the run has been exceptionally chatty, I'm often told, "Hey, you should write those stories down. I learned a lot from hearing that today. Thanks!"

So, a while back, I started to assemble an anthology of running memories and helpful training hints in a folder on my computer labelled *Sweeper Stories*. As the collection grew, I saw a start-to-finish book evolve about going on a journey from not running at all at age forty-eight, to falling in love with trail running in my early fifties, to racing against time on a quest to attempt a 100-mile ultramarathon before I turned sixty. And as the words poured into the manuscript, I discovered strategies for going far—and getting older—that I had not yet articulated for myself: ways of understanding and approaching the great challenges of life revealed through my failures and accomplishments, and the exceptional people I spent trail-time with.

Perhaps Joy is the Reward is the result of that contemplative compilation. It's the story of the physical discoveries I made through the decade of my fifties as I incrementally built up my overall fitness in preparation for the punishment of moving my body 100 continuous miles on my own feet. It's about the mental resilience I gained from repeatedly having to get up after falling along the way. It contains some of the practical lessons I learned over those eleven years: things runners ask me about when they hang with the sweeper at the back of the Saturday morning Capra Trail Running Club. It touches on the mental odds and ends of ultrarunning—and life—and it reveals *what* I believe pulled me out of bed in the twilight hours of all those weekend mornings to run farther and farther distances on mountain trails, and *why* I did that when most others were sleeping in. Finally, *Perhaps Joy is the Reward* tells the story of how reclaiming a finish line lost along the way to my big goal posed the greatest physical and mental challenge of all.

We can get stronger as we get older! *Perhaps Joy is the Reward* is a celebration of that realization and testimony that a late, difficult start is far sweeter than not starting at all.

0 to 100 by 60

The journey I never saw coming.

CHAPTER 1

Going Fast

In late March of 2011, I was a forty-eight-year-old enjoying the last senior men's league hockey game of the winter season. Playing hard, I won a puck battle in the corner, needed to escape by a stride or two to make a clean pass out of the zone, lifted my right skate in anticipation of driving it firmly into the ice and thrusting forward, and instead, drove it down on a pursuing player's stick.

A skate blade on a stick blade on ice is akin to mounting a cannon on grease.

With no bite into the ice, my right leg shot back well beyond its usual extension point with as much power as I could devote to it. My harsh yelp gave instantaneous voice to the jagged, hot explosion of my groin ripping from my pelvis inside my hockey pants.

A few days later, I lay in queasy discomfort on my physiotherapist's treatment bed, afraid she'd prod me where it hurt, and pretty sure I'd injured myself in a way that would severely limit my sporting future—or curtail it entirely.

With a frown, no-nonsense physio Michelle took hold of one of my boney kneecaps, wiggled it back and forth (one of the most annoying and grossest things you can do to me), and said, "You have skinny little runner legs. If you ever want to play hockey again, you're going to have to run to recover from this injury."

"But I haven't run since I was seventeen," I blurted. "My knees are no good."

She tilted her head. Her eyes said *don't be stupid*. Her mouth said, "You play hockey twice a week. You can run."

"Fat guys can play hockey," I argued back. "You don't have to be in shape to play hockey. But you have to be in shape to run."

Fat guys *can* play hockey. Lots of them do. For the average beer league player, skates, reasonably used, give speed and agility that are totally unearned. Also, when you fall on the ice at speed, you don't stop short and jam things, you slide, often injury free. If the boards or other players are close, your equipment protects you when you hit them. All of this, plus the cold rink wind on your face and the hot, rank smell of your sweaty gear, deceive you into thinking you're athletic. It's a gliding, flowing, exhilarating team sport that can be played for years by unfit people. Unless you suddenly have an obliterated groin muscle that precludes the skating reasonably part.

But I wanted to play again, and I trusted Michelle's prescription for recovery, so after a lengthy period of necessary rest, exercises, and agonizing stretches, I dug a pair of heavy, thick-soled runners out from under some junk in the garage. Those runners had to have been from the 80s—there were bugs living in them.

Our neighbourhood was on a north Coquitlam, BC mountainside. Up till that point, I thought the elevated terrain made the place really pretty with its steep roads and high retaining walls that kept the yards from sliding down into each other on the terraced crescents. With buggy bricks laced to my feet, I realized the stacked landscape was pretty awful for running. It was May 13—almost two months into recovery.

I remember walking out the front door with those stiff, old, cumbersome runners on and stopping to think about the hills I would immediately encounter. I turned around and grabbed the truck keys. I drove down to the local park and tried to find a flat spot. I ran. Very briefly. It felt awful. I walked. My lungs burned. I ran again. Feet landed clunky; knees jarred. I was out of breath in seconds, not even minutes. There were no flat spots. I walked more. Nothing about running felt right. I got frustrated. My pelvis ached. And when I climbed back into the truck, I knew I would be back the next day. I had a new project. A challenge. The hook was set. I felt the first tug.

———

It didn't take long to become embarrassed about getting in my truck and driving the few minutes down the hill to the park. Running wasn't supposed to leave a carbon footprint. So, I started running from my front door. After 200 metres of gently rolling sidewalk to the end of our street, I was faced with a decision: uphill or downhill? I chose uphill because that delivered a downhill return at the end, and I needed that to survive.

Never one to start a personal project half-hearted, I settled into a five days per week, thirty minutes per day, running routine—although "running" wasn't the right word at the start. The first 200 metres of up/downs to the end of the street were easy enough to run. The short steep climb after the first left was not. The long gradual ascent up the tree-lined road to the track behind the school was a killer. One kilometre of steady uphill ... and I just could not run the entire distance. Less and less air entered my lungs as I churned up the sidewalk. Out of breath, I would always grind to a stop before reaching the school parking lot. Frustrated by my lack of improvement in the first weeks, and fearing I was too old for this new game, I would walk impatiently past the school and fight to draw a deep breath and fill my lungs. Over and over again, my lungs wouldn't open. I'd walk for a bit and then run/walk and fight for air for the rest of my half-hour outing.

Quitting that repetitiously exhausting running gig entered my mind during many of those asphyxiating shutdowns. To counter that thought, I told myself I was engaged in that breathing battle to help heal and strengthen my groin. But I knew I'd discovered a bigger problem: a complete lack of cardiovascular health. And it was so aggravating to pull hard on a deep breath only to feel like the bottom third of my lungs were glued together.

And then, a month and a half after my first outing in the park, I ran/walked in clunky runners up to the last bump in front of the school, slowed down, drew the longest, deepest, breath I could, and *whammo*, my lungs filled top to bottom.

That sudden sense of having a full reservoir of power was instantly etched in my memory as deeply as the groin tear. A door opened.

I took another deep breath. My lungs filled. Another. And another. *This is real. This is me!* Never had I experienced a physical epiphany of having a switch flip from "I can't physically do this" to "I can do this!" in such a tangible way.

I ran.

The next time out, I turned *right* at the end of our street and headed *down* to the paved trails of our town centre park, 100 vertical metres below our house and just over a kilometre away. Something inside me knew I was going to be able to climb home at the end of my run.

After successive outings that all concluded with successful, though difficult, vertical grinds back up to our front door, the belief that I did indeed have a newfound capacity to go farther, faster, settled on me. Looking back, the ultramarathoner in me was born in those early uphill days. From that point on, I chose the longer, harder way home.

———

All runners know "that person" who, late in a race, comes up silently behind them on a hill and chugs on by as if the incline is insignificant. We loathe "that person."

That person, in this case, "that guy," lived down the street from me. He was my age, the dad of the twins our three kids played with way back when they were all in elementary school. He and I had never spoken more than a "hi" in passing, and as running pushed me out into the neighbourhood, I discovered that his get-out-of-the-house schedule was similar to mine. He was strong on the hills, which miffed me because I had always perceived him as skinny, and not athletic. In the summer of 2011, "that guy" often caught me as I laboured up the last seventy metres of suburban elevation gain that got me home from my expanding repertoire of short flatter routes at the town centre sports park and along the forested Coquitlam River.

One afternoon, as he passed me near the start of our ascent, he strung together more words than I'd ever heard from him. In five one-syllable utterances that dramatically restructured my running mentality, he deadpanned, "This hill is your friend," and chug, chug, chug, up and off he went.

Five words. Impact. In one fleeting moment, "that guy" gave me a new way of thinking. If I wanted to get somewhere rewarding on this new running journey, I had to embrace a new friend: Pain Hill.

———

At age forty-eight, I found myself trying to figure out *how* my body wanted to run. People should just be able to run, right? But my feet didn't land in a way that felt natural. Instead, my foot strikes felt like they went "clunk-clunk" when I ran. My heels hit, clunk, then my knees and hips clunked. My running gait had me rattling like the suspension on an old Trans Am. I feared that all the things they said about running would come true: that I'd wreck my knees and ruin my body and be in agony for all my retirement years. Brought down by a groin injury and finished off by running—the told-you-so crippling of an old guy.

When the frustration level of the clunk-clunk reached its maximum, I'd find myself leaning forward to run on my tippy toes for a while to escape the aggravating heel strike of my high-heeled runners. The out-of-date shoes didn't make landing on the balls of my feet easy, and I could only sustain it for a while before my heels started hitting again, but my natural desire to get forward on my feet interested me. It felt like my body was teasing me with a solution.

And because it roused my curiosity, what did I do? I researched it.

Didn't take long to figure out that there might be more running information on the web than cat videos. Also didn't take long for me to figure out that I was a forefoot striker, not a heel striker, and that my old bug-infested runners with the oversized sponge cake heels were my nemesis. And I learned a term that in 2011 was relatively new: zero drop—a phrase coined by Golden Harper who co-founded Altra, a running shoe company that focused on footwear with no elevation difference from heel to toe. My problem was that in those early zero-drop days, I couldn't get my hands on a pair of Altras anywhere!

In mid-July, I went down to the local sports store and bought a pair of flat-soled matte-black New Balance Minimus runners. Road slippers was how I described them. Zero clunk described the way they worked for me. I got home and ran "Minimus-ly" down my street and felt as light on my forefeet as Legolas of the Woodland Realm. My running gait was smooth. My heels did feathery touch-and-goes with the ground. I felt like a kid running in bare feet. That was my first lesson in figuring out how my body wanted to work, and then getting the right running gear to support its needs. The heels on those road slippers, and every subsequent pair of zero-drop road running shoes I owned, were retired into the garbage bin in pristine condition, even though the toe boxes and front soles were beat to crap.

———

Directly linked to my improved running form, my cardiorespiratory fitness was improving too. My running strength was slowly building as well, thanks to my new friend, Pain Hill. And let me be perfectly clear on this point, I was not running up that hill. I was fast hiking it as consistently as I could. That was hard enough in the early days.

My next hurdle was being able to sustain a running pace—no walking at all—for 5 kilometres. I just couldn't do it.

Twenty minutes into a run, my lungs started burning, or my leg muscles hurt too much, or my side stitched up, or I mentally gave in to the urge to walk a bit and breathe deeply because it felt so good. My journal notes are consistent through June and July that first summer of running: "22 min run. 2 walk / 2 run to finish." "24 min run. Walk/run." Entry after entry.

Then, on August 12, I ran 5 kilometres on a flat route that took me from the park to Eagle Ridge Hospital, where Cindy worked, and back, in twenty-nine minutes with no walking. I had not set out with a plan to do such a thing. *Where did that come from?* Only three months earlier, I'd stuffed my feet into the buggy clodhoppers from the 80s for the first time. I'd progressed from not running at all, to being able to run a half-hour 5K.

Six days later, I ran my first full 10 kilometres—no walking— in under an hour. I had a hard time comprehending what my body had just done. The one-week jump from 5 to 10 kilometres was an exponential improvement when compared to the three aggravating months of baby steps that preceded it. I was overjoyed by my progress, but unable to explain how my body had made the big leap. I hadn't done a single special exercise or eaten any magic vegetables.

All I knew was that my mind wasn't in charge on either of those runs. I went along for the ride—like being in the car with my kids the first few weeks they were learning how to drive. I just knew, with a tight grip on the seat, that the car was driving them—and me. I was an incompetent runner merrily blazing along with my body leading the way and my conscious mind trying to catch up to what was turning on deep inside.

I stepped back on the ice on September 26 in much better physical condition than when I entered the rink for my rip-roaring season finale the previous March. The injury site on my pelvis felt fragile when I increased thrust on my skating stride, and my belief that I wouldn't re-injure myself was what required the most strengthening in the early games. In the big picture, I'd done more than get back to playing hockey through that summer of learning to run—I'd gained a whole new game. Implemented as a temporary mechanism for rehab, running turned out to be something I couldn't release after it successfully delivered me to the place where I initially assumed I'd be glad to part ways with it.

———

Seven months later, on the morning of April 15, 2012, I stood on Georgia Street in downtown Vancouver, BC, with 48,903 other runners. Not exactly a quaint gathering of like-minded individuals, although there was an intimacy associated with being squished like jarred pickles into our finish-time corrals. It was a warmer-than-usual day for mid-April. I had flat-soled road slippers on my feet and was appropriately apparelled in new black running shorts and blue sweat-wicking tee. But regardless of how well I appeared to fit in, I felt like an imposter in the one-hour corral. I'd run that distance in less than an hour many times by that point, but standing there, with all those thousands of *real* runners, one big question persisted: *Was I truly one of these people?*

My guess was that my wife Cindy, crammed into her own corral nearby with her perpetually youthful face bright beneath her runner's cap and thick ponytail of long wavy salt-and-pepper hair bobbing this way and that, felt fine. A sprint triathlon competitor in her mid-thirties, Cindy had fallen off the fitness wagon along with me as we moved toward our forties.

At age thirty-four, I was the first to become unfit and over-weight when I moved from a physical life in the construction industry to one of endless lunches and dinners associated with international business travel, and the sit-and-type screen time hours required for managing a high-tech distribution network around North America and Europe. That was during my OMNEX Control Systems career; thirteen special years with a blossom-ing radio-control engineering company out of Port Coquitlam, BC; a time in my life when I learned to lead, and where expo-sure to a wide variety of professionals and cultures broadened my mind.

At age forty, Cindy had traded in her fitness hours for study hours when she headed back to school at Douglas College in Burnaby, BC, to acquire the registered nursing degree she by-passed when our family started early. During those years, I was on the road for three months out of twelve, Cindy was study-ing for her degree, our oldest daughter, Krystina, was at Simon Fraser University preparing for her teaching career, and Phillip and Jeanette, our two youngest children, were making their way through high school. Through all of that, physical fitness remained on the low rungs of our priority list until 2008, when I departed OMNEX to become a work-from-home Great Clips franchisee, and Cindy graduated as a registered nurse.

With lives and free time a little more under control, our health renaissance slowly took shape. A bit more time in the gym for Cindy. Some weightlifting in our basement for me. Getting bikes to ride for pleasure and to work. Then came my injury. I learned to run, and Cindy, seeing the joy it brought me, got moving again too. For her, the Vancouver Sun Run corral was not a new experience—it was a welcome return to the world of community athletic events. For me, it was a scary next step.

I took two things from the 2012 Sun Run. The first was ethereal: the sound of nearly 100,000 feet softly padding the pavement, reverberating in that narrow, downtown, concrete canyon— loud enough, due to sheer number, to be shocking. Four blocks in, I had about half the runners ahead and half behind me. There were no voices, just the hushed rumble of myriad footfalls. I was deeply moved by a collective sense of humanity. We sounded, and felt, like one flowing river. The second was instructional: over and over, a group of runners (maybe in their early twenties), would tear by me, elbows out, rude as hell, faces grimacing like they were in a death race and could only survive by winning the thing, and then I would catch up to find them standing with hands on hips, heaving for breath, still grimacing. Minutes later, they'd elbow past me again only to be found standing half a kilometre down the road. Idiots. They gave me my first annoying lesson in incorrect pacing.

Successfully running the elbow rapids on Vancouver's wondrous river of humanity, I sailed across the finish line of the first sanctioned race event of my life. Finish time 00:56:07. In less than ninety days, I would turn fifty. Google pegged the average male fifty-year-old 10K finish time at 00:56:12. Nailed it. One year in, I was officially an average road runner.

———

Up until 2012, roads in my life were for driving, and trails were for hiking. From a trail that passed directly behind our house, we had direct access to hundreds of kilometres of trails across Eagle and Burke Mountains and along the Coquitlam River that ran between them. Regrettably, by 2012 we had already lived on that forest trail network for twenty years, and I had seldom used it.

Cindy was much better at getting out on those trails with our dogs: Taya, an eight-year-old Nova Scotia Duck Toller, and Kahlua, a four-year-old golden retriever. And to Cindy goes all the credit for the turn our lives took when she looked up from her laptop one day and said, "You know, you don't have to run on the road all the time; you can run on the trails. There's a trail racing series called 5 Peaks that has family-friendly running events all across Canada with really cool races that are 5-to-7 kilometres long. There are five of them right around here that I'd really like to try." She spun the laptop my way. "Check it out."

Our newfound running focus had made an important impact on our marriage at that point. As our nest emptied with the kids moving out and Phil, then Krystina, getting married, Cindy's and my joint sporting life was reborn after a long hiatus. In our twenties, Cindy and I had occasionally golfed together until our weekends filled with kids' activities. Thereafter, my aversion to swimming—stone in water—led to me having zero urge to participate in Cindy's triathlons in our thirties. Hockey was my twice-a-week sport. Given our different interests, I've wondered how our lives together would have played out in the decade of our fifties if our sudden common interest in running, and then the trail community, hadn't dovetailed into each of us supporting the other's sporting and fitness aspirations. Rather than drift apart when the kids left, we became laced together by our trail shoes.

I immediately said yes to her signing us up for the 5 Peaks BC Alice Lake Sport Course that June. It was exciting but concerning too. We were registered for our first trail race date, and I didn't have a clue what to wear.

A number of years earlier, on a wintry ridge trail above our neighbourhood, I was strenuously hiking in my thick-soled hiking boots, wool socks and heavy pants, and a pack stuffed with all the emergency supplies that were necessary for the deep dark woods (less than 2 kilometres from our doorstep and within crawling distance of rescue), and of course, a toque, gloves, and jacket with the zipper open wide because I was sweating. I was the consummate over-dressed, over-prepared tourist/hiker poster boy who, from time to time, pretended to live the Himalayan expedition life I read about in mountaineering books. On those rare days of adventure play, I was the portly Canadian embodiment of George Mallory, or perhaps Sir Edmund Hillary, or maybe even Tenzing Norgay.

Carefully studying where I'd plant each foot as I ascended, I startled to the sound of an animal rushing toward me from above. Fight, not flight, fully activated, I crouched and shouted an unspellable word at the attacking beast that was on me fast. It was a phantom of leggy flesh and bare arms clad in short shorts and a T-shirt—in the winter! It moved like a gazelle, nimbly hopping at breakneck speed from rock to rock, small stones clattering where its feet briefly touched down. "Hey buddy!" the aberration called happily as it shot past. I think it waved, its open-mouthed smile all teeth.

Dumbstruck, I watched it speed away. Seconds later, a black dog tore by me in pursuit.

I had sighted my first trail runner. I thought he was a complete fool. Insane. Totally going to get himself killed. Who would run down a hill like that, half-naked in the cold? I told funny stories about that guy for years.

As Cindy clicked the register button with a mischievous, *Here we go!* look on her face, I thought of the phantom and wondered what I should wear to my first trail race—a real quandary. From the road running we'd been doing, I had some ideas for covering my uppers and lowers, though not as thinly as the phantom, but where the rubber would meet the road—or rather, dirt—was a big concern. Those feather-light minimal sole runners I was skipping around the roads with were not cutting it on mildly rocky paths, and I knew they weren't going to offer any protection on a race called "5 Peaks."

So, believe it or not, I went down into the garage again and managed to dig out another pair of clunky running shoes with big grippy things on the bottoms. I have no idea where or why I bought those hideous runners. They were still in their original box. No bugs. With green, octopus-like suction nodules adorning the soles, and translucent sparkle fluid in exposed futuristic cushion sacks under the heels, they looked to me like they would give me the traction, support, and protection I needed on my first mountain race. I laced them on, ran to the trail behind our back fence, and headed up to my "legends of Everest" route on our neighbourhood hill. There, on the meandering dirt paths in the trees, I gave myself a crash course in how to be that guy I joked about.

To say the trail runners in the starting pen of the 5 Peaks Alice Lake 7K Sport Course race were curious about my green "trail" running shoes would be an understatement. So many questions about make, model, and function, and I had no answers. "Yeah, these are my trail shoes," was about all I could say. I could tell that some people thought I was somehow ahead of the curve, and they were perturbed that I wouldn't tell them more about my never-been-seen-before gear, because surely that old guy must know what he was doing. *Oh my.*

Saved from a slipped-and-fell calamity by my too-heavy octo-grip squishy-heeled greenies, and wearing old weighty shorts that ran a little tight in the crotch, plus a top I profusely sweated in because a body running on mountain trails was a furnace, swinging a too-tiny handheld water bottle, I became a trail racer on June 9, 2012, three weeks before I turned fifty.

Having decided we'd run the race at whatever pace felt good to us individually, Cindy and I split up in the starting corral, and I went out of the gate fast, excited to be with runners darting along the lush green forest paths. The first steep set of vertical switch-

backs cut into the mossy damp stone delivered a startling revelation: trail runners hiked hills. The elite runners scampered on
ahead, but the majority hiked upward at speed—some with arms
sweeping like dangling metronomes, others with palms pressed
down into their thighs, each strong step driving them uphill. I
could not keep pace with the racers who powered up the mountainside with long, even walking strides. I was amazed by the way
the slower group I stayed with shifted gears on different terrain.
Movement on the trail was nothing like the repetitious pounding
of road running. Instead, it was the art of body mechanics flowing,
leaping, stutter-stepping, hands-gripping-trees-to-make-a-corner
motion. I was astonished by the way I was able to navigate the
trippy root-entwined downhill sections with reasonable rapidity.
Yet again, the unconscious runner in me was at work, taking my
body places my conscious mind would not have gotten it to go
with forethought, if at all. *I was the phantom!*

Rather than feeling like an oddball out of my element, I was
enthralled to be part of a group of people running in the mountain
forest. From the moment we arrived at the registration tent, Cindy
and I just fit in (which spoke volumes about the 5 Peaks organiza-
tion and the participants).

After the race, Cindy and I felt so welcome we didn't want to
leave. We wanted to enjoy that unique community. Yes, it was a
much smaller bunch than the 48,904 at the Vancouver Sun Run,
about 333 times smaller, but the people were just, well, really
nice, and I didn't sense any egos . . . or experience any elbows.
There was a sense that I'd stumbled into a comfortable group of
my people—a group I never knew existed before. There was an
instant connection.

We hung out for a long while to watch the awards ceremonies
and mingle with folks who randomly greeted us. We browsed the
vendor tents (where I saw real trail shoes), and I did something
that made another profound impact on my nascent running life: I

checked out a sheet taped to the silver gear trailer with everyone's race times printed on it.

Randy Klassen, M40-49, 12/28. Twelfth place out of twenty-eight runners in that bracket.

Huh. Middle of the pack again, even though I was almost fully aged out of my bracket. *Cool.*

Then I looked at the M50-59 bracket. *Shut the front door!* If I had run that exact race all over again after my birthday in three weeks, I would have been on the podium in third place, as a fifty-year-old!

Ping!

In that instant, I had my first running goal: a place I would consciously strive to take myself, instead of just following my body down the road. I was going to podium a 5 Peaks trail race at age fifty.

On June 15, 2012, I ran the UBC Longest Day Road Race 10K—time 00:47:58. Thirty-fifth out of 117 in the M40-49 bracket. I was sixteen days shy of my fiftieth birthday and performing better than average. In the days after the Alice Lake race, I second-guessed my performance there and wondered if that quick run might have been a lucky one-off, but this positive result at my old alma mater gave impetus to the notion that I could be fast in the forest. A running project with an audacious goal was a definite possibility.

For some reason, four weeks after I ran a 20-kilometre out-and-back on the river trails. Not sure what inspired that—in my journal notes, it's totally out of place—but that day, something motivated me to push that distance. Clearly, my confidence and stamina were improving.

On October 18, 2012, I ran the Granville Island Turkey Trot 10K—time 00:48:51. I was getting faster than the average turkey, and, at fifty years of age, I was excited about getting faster and stronger than I'd ever been.

———

2013 turned out to be the fastest year of my life on the running side of the equation. On the business side, I ground out six of the longest, most toilsome months I had ever crawled through.

The stage was set for those tough months back when I left OMNEX to become a franchisee and partner with my long-time friend, Mark Tucker, who played an instrumental role in bringing Great Clips family-oriented hair salons into Canada in the early 90s. Having decided to turn their fifteen years of Great Clips success into significance, Mark and his wife, Shirly, returned in 2007 to South Africa, where they had grown up and started their family, to found the Phakamani Foundation, a micro-lending non-profit that empowered women in the townships to start and grow their own businesses to pull themselves, their families, and their communities out of poverty. Mark and Shirly's departure from Canada left their Great Clips salons in the very capable hands of General Manager Sam Bolic, but Sam was so busy managing existing salons that he had no time to build new salons, something that remained vital to Mark, and Great Clips. That's where I came in. In late 2008, I was to be the builder with the goal of expanding our locations, and our Canadian success, and thereby continue to enhance Phakamani's impact abroad.

When the cyclical Alberta economy boomed again after the 2009 bust, I played my role and commuted back and forth between Greater Vancouver and Edmonton to build and open at least two Great Clips hair salons a year. The demand to service the high-paid workers pouring into Alberta to fill positions in the petroleum trades—with trendy fade cuts that didn't get messed by their hard-hats—was real. In an attempt to capture that underserved market, the bulk of my construction efforts were focused there, and once the new salons were operational, I general-managed those teams as well.

Then, in 2013, following four non-stop years of growth and expansion, the province ran out of service industry workers needed to fulfill the employment requirements of hundreds, if not thousands, of new businesses that had opened in the retail, food, and personal services sectors. I completed our beautiful, bright, high-ceilinged flagship hair salon in the burgeoning Currents of Windermere destination shopping centre at the start of May 2013—our seventh new store in three and a half years. Without staff to operate it, the lights remained off. At the end of the month, our construction loan, rent, and tax obligations had to be met. We weren't alone. Several freshly built stores remained dark around us too. The competition for employees was vicious. Workers jumped from job to job, grasping for the next highest wage offer. Not only was it difficult to find new stylists for our newest salon, but we were also fighting to retain our existing staff from being poached by construction companies offering exorbitant wages to road flaggers. Stylists became pilot vehicle operators driving for trucking companies paying astronomical rates. It was a cash-infused economy in a frenzy.

After locking the doors on a new business where customers pulled up continually to find no employees inside, I flew home and poured my frustrations into running the BMO Vancouver Half Marathon 21.1K in a time of 1:52:51. Google said the average time for a beginner fifty-year-old was 2:42:27; intermediate 1:56:04. Wearing minty-green flat-soled road slippers, skimpy black running shorts I wouldn't have been caught dead in two years earlier, and a blue running tee that became my good luck shirt for many years, I flew the initial downhill from Queen Elizabeth Park and headed toward the stark, jutting high-rise Vancouver skyline backdropped by the sea-hazed North Shore Mountains. I kept the burners on through historic China Town, slowed along sparkling English Bay, afloat with freighters at anchor, then picked up my pace as runners knotted in Stanley Park's tighter city-forest pathways where the urge to *beat that guy* and *get ahead of that pack* took hold.

No, I didn't win the race. No, I wasn't super-fast. I was middle-of-the-pack fast. But winning wasn't about being first. That day winning was beating the irritating person who bragged too loudly in the corral. It was beating my own expectations. It was finishing a race when I couldn't finish something else in life, and that alone was the most meaningful win I could have had. I revelled in it. Finishing well at the BMO Half was a far cry better than chaining up the doors on a brand-new business.

I've never liked to leave things unfinished. I was never one to sit and cry about the predicaments I found myself in. On repeated trips to Edmonton that summer, I scoured the city for employees by day, and ran the clay earthen-smelling North Saskatchewan River Valley Trails in the evenings. I failed miserably between eight and five, then I pushed myself to succeed on the trails by nightfall. Reaching distance targets. Exceeding time targets. Achieving something rather than nothing. Running kept me healthy and motivated during hours when I could have sat alone and fretted and guzzled beer. Running in 2013 lent order to my chaos. Being out in the woods with Cindy and the dogs when I was home gave me peace.

Running that year also gave me a project with structured steps toward a tangible goal: to podium at the 5 Peaks races and in the season series. Unlike the previous year when my first milestone distance achievements like 5K, 10K, and 20K took me by surprise, in 2013, my running distances and targets were integrated into an overall plan, and part of executing that plan was to sign up for the BMO Vancouver Half with the goal of training to run it as fast as I could to build strength, speed, and endurance to nail the shorter 5 Peaks races that would follow through the summer.

———

Typically, people who earn their podium finishes know right away where they stand in their races—they get to the finish line and there is no one else around. When you think about it like that, winning outright could be viewed as a lonely thing.

I'm joking. I've been close to dead last in a few races. That's lonely.

Loneliness was not in store for me on June 8, 2013, when I returned to run the 5 Peaks Alice Lake Sport Course for the second year with a goal in mind and a pair of bona fide Saucony Peregrine trail running shoes on my feet. Off the start, younger, stronger athletes passed me on the tall-treed uphill switchbacks and on the more level ground contoured to the eye by tree shadow and sunlight. Higher up, I passed timid runners carefully picking their way down rocky sections slick with the grime of hundreds of racing feet. As I neared the finish, the sounds of the already boisterous party swelled whenever race announcer John Crosby called out finisher names to cheers that boomed above his eclectic music mix. I was surrounded by lively and spirited heavy breathers the whole way.

So, I made Cindy, who was cooling off after her own exhilarating run, wait with me for that sheet to be taped to the gear trailer to see where I landed with the old guys who I didn't see much of out on the course. I admit, my stomach convulsed as I paced around, pretending to be interested in things other than that trailer, making idle chat with Cindy, who found my poorly disguised intensity a bit much. Not knowing who I was competing against among all those runners, whose ages I continually guessed wrong, left me completely in the dark about where I stood versus whom. Then the results went up.

Hot damn! Second place in the M50-59 bracket! Podium!
Oh, the power of having a plan!

Funny how stepping forward out of the crowd to rise and stand on that wooden box, just a little higher than the mob, able to look down on everyone but the guy on the centre box, made me feel like a superhero. I had never experienced a winning athletic moment like that in my entire life. The glazed pottery "2nd" that hung around my neck was fulfilling in a giddy little boy way. And I felt so very encouraged by the community. Not in a "Hey, you're great, man!" kind of way, but in a "Way to go, well earned!" kind of way. There was a big difference between the two. The sense of genuine support went along with seeing the winners and elite runners, some of them in the rattiest gear, cheering the stragglers at the end. Their authentic humbleness all made that new trail-running gang shine a little more brightly in my life.

Second place that day was definitely number one for me.

Focused on keeping the speed up, I returned to the UBC Longest Day Race five weeks later and put up a time of 00:46:51 on the 10K, two weeks shy of turning fifty-one. That was officially the fastest my body had ever moved over a reasonable distance, self-propelled. I'll never know what I could have achieved if I had become a runner at a younger age.

Through the first four races of the 2013 5 Peaks BC series, I finished second, fourth, fourth, and fourth. I also got to know who my competition was—and liked all of them, even though their better efforts kept pushing me off those battered wooden boxes. As the fifth and final race approached, I had my eye on the overall standings because some of the other guys on the leaderboard weren't quite as consistent as me, except for Mr. First Place, Gordon Flett, who was competitive at an elite level and finished well ahead of all the rest of us each race. The math told me that if I finished second in the last race of the season, I could vault myself onto the race series podium too. Game on. The finale would decide the series.

The September 28 5 Peaks Buntzen Lake race was my best flat-out footrace. The first 6 kilometres were a stride-for-stride, back-and-forth duel for second place. Two older guys with families and work lives and lawns to be mowed, duking it out on the climbs and descents of a rainy, lakeside forest trail. We were serious about it that day. Second place was first place in both of our minds because Mr. First Place would never be caught.

Though I trailed on all the ascents through the first 5 kilometres, I had the lead by mere metres when we pounded across the undulating suspension bridge at the far end of the lake, and after that, my competitor faded. I wish our battle had continued another 4 kilometres to the end. It was exhilarating while it lasted and intense to be pursued, like fleeing a predator, but for real, not in a dream. There was something viscerally life or death about that chase on a cold, wet mountain trail.

Two freezing podiums in a downpour ended the 5 Peaks 2013 season. I stepped up onto the number two box for the race and the number two box for the series. Of equal, or greater, importance, the moving, fleeing, and chasing in the forest that got me there gave me life.

Much to our surprise, Cindy's name was called for third place in the F40-49 bracket season awards. Cindy was rewarded for showing up to each and every race and getting across the finish lines that year. Her perseverance put her, the slower consistent one, on the podium with the two rabbits who had raced each other all season. Cindy's surprising award was a highlight and spoke the loudest about why we were out there: to push ourselves into new territory and be rewarded with the unforeseen. In a way, it also set the stage for how I would change my approach to trail racing. Going forward, I would seek my rewards in long-distance tenacity, rather than short, sprinted victory.

———

After a long string of financial losses, hard-fought hires, and a painful partial opening in September, we staged a Christmas grand opening for the Great Clips I had finished building seven months earlier. Festive customers poured in. A much-needed win for our young manager, Kaitlin, who bore the tension that came from serving too many customers with too few stylists for too many months, and for her grand opening team that survived those trial-by-fire weeks. To watch that new location stretch its wings in good health was a long-awaited relief for us as owners, too.

That New Year, I leafed through the underlined sentences and margin notes in the books I'd read in 2013 to review what I had learned about business, running, the nature of our world, and myself. I also looked back at my personal and business decisions and, while reflecting on what went right and wrong, I took note of how two major passions in my life were integrating. Was I empowered to win that late September footrace for second place by having managed to get a store partway open and limping along at the start of September? How much self-assurance did squeezing results from that summer of perseverance give? And did the confidence I gained from fighting that running duel on the trails with another old guy inspire me to continue fighting to achieve that Christmas grand opening too? What did all those accomplishments do for my psyche? Was I a better franchisee at the end of 2013 than I was the year before because trail running was changing me? Was I a better athlete because of the way my business struggles had toughened me? Had I become an athlete? I saw that everything in 2013 was connected. It all worked together.

CHAPTER 2

Going Far

At the beginning of 2014, I took stock of where my running game might go. I was halfway through fifty-one. That left me with eight and a half years in the 50-59 age bracket. I knew monotony would overtake me if I kept running the same races with the same competition over and over, waiting for the young guns to push me off my newfound podiums. I'd never been good at repetition, I was project oriented with a bent for creating and building new things, so I sought out my next challenge: I opted to go far. The new plan—more like a gamble at that point—was to test myself against a monster I'd discovered in the trail running magazines: a very long trail race known as an ultramarathon.

An ultramarathon is generally defined as any race longer than a 26.2-mile (42.2-kilometre) marathon, and they are most often trail races over a wide variety of terrain (forests, mountains, deserts etc.) with little or no paved road running. Typical ultra-distances are 50K, 50-miles, 100K, 100-miles, and then a whole variety of distances beyond that depending on the event type and the craziness of the runners—or level of commitment. Where many road runners see race distance progression as 5K to 10K to a half-marathon to the holy grail of the full marathon, ultrarunners enter the game at 50K with a longing eye on the finisher buckles associated with the 100-something distances. To put this in perspective, a 100-miler is four marathons strung together over difficult wilderness terrain, thereby earning the prefix "ultra."

With no more than a half-marathon under my belt at that point, I figured I should complete a full marathon before going ultra, so I signed up for the May 2014 BMO Vancouver Marathon Full 42.2K. That would be my gateway to the mountainous and tough Squamish50K (SQ50K) in August. The increased mileage of both races and the elevation gain/loss of the SQ50K would require a massive training commitment. Colossal. But feeling like a winner with three 5 Peaks medals dangling off the shelf above my work computer, I laid my money down on the not-cheap entry fees and bet on myself to successfully go far on the single-track of the coastal mountains.

Thirty-five years earlier, two friends and I had hiked a portion of the Rocky Mountains' Great Divide outside of Jasper, Alberta in the summer between grades eleven and twelve. Those five days comprised the only entry in my mountain adventure-guy re-sume. Getting out on far-flung trails and going ultra would be my uncharted journey to the world's end and beyond—leaps and bounds beyond my pre-5 Peaks huffing and puffing on a local hill nestled safely in a city subdivision. Life changing.

———

Shortly after signing up for my long-distance races, I smashed up my ribs and sternum in a full-speed on-ice collision with a fellow teammate back at the rink where I continued to "cross train" for my new running gig. Oh, to have video of that one. Puck squirted out of our zone—past two opposing defencemen trapped flat-footed at our blueline—and tumbled with speed toward centre ice and beyond. Teammate Marty and I were both in positions to chase it from opposite sides of the ice, and together we launched in a tandem race to catch it. Each of us picked up speed as we flew across centre ice, and then, not wanting to put our fellow team-mate offside, we each succumbed to over-generosity and made the lightning decision to give our buddy the breakaway. The result: a stupendous connection as Marty and I simultaneously banked from our flight paths and swooped directly toward each other. I, with my head up, saw Marty, who was supposed to shoot past, instead turn directly into me with his head down. Then I felt his helmet in my chest. In the next instant, I was looking down at my skates, but beneath them, far away, were the rafters of the rink ceiling, an indication that I was flying through the air upside down.

In the end, I did not recall my landing. I did recall my amazement that Marty's neck wasn't broken. I also recalled that after both teams figured out we were going to live, they couldn't stop laughing at our ridiculous collision. I could only imagine what it looked like from the goalie's perspective: two guys madly racing toward him, then suddenly smashed together at his blueline by forces unseen.

"Herbert," I said to our family doctor a few days later, "I'm heading into a big training period for my first marathon. Can I keep running with cracked ribs?"

"It's just pain," Herbert replied. "Not like you're going to hurt them more." Our good doctor never pampered us; he just dealt out the facts. I wondered how that went over with his wife and kids, who we had got to know at band concerts and school graduations shared with our kids over the preceding decades.

It turned out that I could run and push out distances in training with messed up ribs. Herbert was right; it was just pain. The cracks healed as I carried on with my five day per week running routine. It also turned out that executing my first marathon on a bitterly cold May 4, 2014 would introduce me to a concept I knew nothing about: fuelling for a long race.

"Where is the food?!" I angrily demanded after I crossed the finish line, forty-four minutes past my goal time of four hours. Not something a smartly trained and competent marathon runner should utter. It was obvious that I did not know my body's needs beyond 30 kilometres—my longest training run prior to that race.

That day I also learned an important lesson in humility that would guide my future training.

Waiting for the start of the race in the four-hour finish time corral, I did what all runners do: looked around and sized up my competition. No matter how casual the runner, they are lying if they tell you they never ask themselves, *Who do I think I can beat?*

The answer to that question, as I was about to learn, wasn't always obvious. Some people who looked very fit were slow or lacked stamina; some who had body types rarely portrayed in the athletic literature back in 2014 moved surprisingly fast or had great stamina. As I scanned the corral, I saw a group of runners that I immediately pegged as able to have fun in short races (like the family-oriented races I'd been exposed to), but definitely unable to finish a marathon. Having never run a marathon before, in my mind their body types did not equate with the distance challenge we all faced. In fact, when I looked at myself in the mirror that morning and saw skimpily dressed muffin-topped me, I questioned my own athleticism.

What are they doing in this corral? I thought to myself. *I mean, kudos to them for showing up and hoping to get to the end of this thing . . . but the four-hour corral?*

On the backside of Stanley Park, I got schooled.

About 35 kilometres into the 42-kilometre race, I was a mess—full-on lethargic due to improper fuelling (bonking, as runners say) and frozen beyond discomfort in the unexpected wind and driving rain that rendered my rain shell useless. My legs were cramping severely because of improper hydration and electrolyte management, and worst of all ... I was walking. Me, the fast guy, walking to the end, miserable.

That's when the happy, laughing, talking-a-mile-a-minute, group that "would only have fun on short races" ran by me.

Ran by me.

They weren't running fast. Their pace was not quick. But they weren't walking either.

Neither were they running smooth and easy—like I strove to do. Better than that, they were each running in a fashion that suited their individual body design, and I bet they'd been running that pace right from the start when I'd shot out ahead of them. I bet they were also running at that pace when they crossed the finish line way the heck ahead of me—the guy who was no longer running.

Their pace management performance was impactful.

Never again did I make a critical judgment about anyone's speed, strength, or endurance capabilities based on looks. Ultimately, that experience also drove home the point that I needed to build training and fuelling plans that suited my body type rather than blindly adopting online plans made for bodies with muscles and digestion peculiarities that weren't mine. I needed to get specific—like the members of that successful run group who were all probably on their way home by the time I dragged myself over the line.

Not only did my first full road marathon leave me feeling embarrassed, slow, and incapable of going long distances, it also left me hobbled.

Mile after mile of pounding the pavement over four months of focused training had left me with brand new pains in my left knee … and the perfect excuse to back out of my first ultramarathon slated for August. My huge bonk at the 30-kilometre mark left me uncertain about how to manage my fuelling. My aching knee, which sometimes squeezed out fireballs of pain, scared me. So I dropped down from the Squamish50K to the 23-kilometre SQ23 race that Cindy had trained for, and together we ran our first big mountain race as a team.

We had a wonderful day and ran/hiked the multi-canopied rainforest course in tandem, step for step, with a finish time of

4:09:00—ironically, or perhaps not, my full road marathon goal time on a mountain half-marathon. The implications for what ultramarathoning would demand of my body and mental capacity were not lost on me.

The Squamish50 weekend in August of 2014 charmed us. Those single-track trails, the volunteers, John Crosby the ever-present southwestern BC race announcer, the finish line all-day parties, and race directors Gary Robbins and Geoff Langford were all affixed in our hearts. Little did Cindy and I know when we crossed that first sunny Saturday finish line, with John loudly teasing me on the mic about my bright red Altra Lone Peak trail running shoes, that thousands of training kilometres and hundreds of hours would be dedicated in the coming years to striving to conquer each race distance the Squamish50 offered, and that tremendous joy would be derived from volunteering and cheering, and sharing beers, and laughing and crying in the rocks and forests and muck and finish line grass of that place.

In between the BMO Vancouver Full Marathon and our SQ23 day, I returned to the UBC Longest Day Race and put up a time of 00:52:52. I didn't quite run that 10K in the number of minutes of my age (a competitive mark for those over thirty-five) and didn't care. I was going longer now. There would be no more podiums. I was choosing to race against myself ... and the cutoff clock.

Looking back, getting a coach was an option at that point, but I was too autodidactic and independent to submit to a running boss. Instead, I resorted to immersing myself in ultrarunning books, magazines, and web resources. I also started paying attention to gear specifically designed for the sport at Distance Runwear, a new store owned by local running expert Dave Cressman. My goal was to run an ultramarathon, and after being exposed to the energy and camaraderie of our first ultramarathon weekend at the Squamish50 races, I was more determined than ever to learn how to do it.

——

One year, numerous local races, and well over 1,000 training kilometres later, in August of 2015, I stood shivering with nervousness in the starting corral of my first ultramarathon, the Squamish50K. Ahead of me lay 8,500 feet of vertical gain and 9,000 feet of descent across a rainforest mountain course described online as "an exceptionally difficult course made tougher still by the technical nature of a majority of the terrain. Throw in the fact that the back half runs much more difficult than the front half, and you have yourself a nice little day of suffering."

I wanted a challenge. I got one—with a cutoff time limit of eleven and a half hours.

In the months leading up to the race, I also got imaginative with my pre-big-run-injury theme and let a rotting molar fester in my head for much too long before having it, and part of my lower right jaw, surgically removed five weeks before my 50K. The surgeon packed the hole with stinky granular bits of cadaver bone that floated loose for weeks. It wasn't a hockey injury, but it was as significant as any break, or sprain, or ligament tear I'd ever had. It's just that it was my face, not my legs, *So why worry, right?*

I asked the surgeon if I could finish training for my upcoming ultra. He said no.

I scaled back to meet his demand and ran 44, 63, and 66 kilometres respectively in the three weeks before my taper (which also happened to be the three weeks after my surgery). Looking back, I'm pretty sure my bad behaviour was why those bad-tasting bits of cadaver bone kept surfacing through the stitch holes in my gums instead of mending themselves into nice new bone where I needed it. Probably also the reason why I had to get the surgery redone five months later to keep my jaw from falling apart. *Oops. Who knew that surgery was actually injury and not just pain?*

The Squamish50K. Let's just say it lived up to its billing, and I learned how extreme ultrarunning was. To compare a 50K mountain ultra to a 5K road race would be like telling a fisherman staring down a typhoon that he was about to experience moisture.

The emotive power of standing in that lakeside starting corral, looking up to the dawn-lit mountains that would resist all my efforts to conquer them over the coming 50 kilometres, with a time cutoff, was exquisite. The endlessness of the climbs. The brutality of the technical descents down the breakneck mountain bike trails. The muscle pain and mental fatigue. The determination required to not just catch a ride home from the last aid station where Cindy consoled me and our daughters Krystina and Jeanette said, "Dad, you got this," was life-changing—as cliché as that may be.

I spontaneously cried atop the Mountain of Phlegm Trail when I realized I had 5 kilometres to go and was going to make the race finish cutoff time without any heroic efforts; I did not have the strength to run one more step over those last kilometres. As I walked it in, sobs welled up again when I heard the finish line cheers in the distance. It was the sound of the chorus of humans that staggered me emotionally. Overcome by the feeling of having fought and survived a punishing, lonely battle, the sounds of my family, friends, and trail clan, now within reach, felt, in a word, *safe*. I cried as if I was about to be saved.

In a state that altered how I viewed myself and my capabilities, I earned my first ultramarathon medal—goal accomplished. I'd heard athletes say, "I left it all out there." Persevering through hours of toilsome climbing and descending, bearing the pain of an angry IT band that destroyed my running stride, choosing not to quit when all I could do was walk, and getting my hobbling self to the SQ50K finish line took me far beyond my previous physical and mental borders and showed me what "leaving it all out there" really felt like. After I crossed over the final timing strip, and got my medal, and my first ultra-hug from red-bearded Race Director

Gary Robbins, I lurched around on stiff, aching legs and celebrated with Krystina and her husband Joel, and Jeanette who ran her first SQ23 with Cindy that day and blew off both her big toenails in that stony battle. We savoured burgers that dripped with exertion-amplified taste. We cheered the final beaten-down finishers—I cried again for a few of them too. And when the day drew to a close, I didn't think I had it in me to go farther, let alone ever do it again.

Until a few weeks later, of course, when I didn't know what to do with myself without a big running project ahead of me. In September, I signed up for another 50K ultra taking place in March of 2016. Being hooked on running evolved into being hooked on ultrarunning, despite the suffering ... or maybe because the hook itself was the heightened emotional experience of overcoming that suffering. Having crossed a threshold into a new world of self-awareness, the urge to explore it began to well up like a lost memory of who I really was.

———

That October, Cindy, Jeanette, and I travelled to Nepal to celebrate Jeanette's successful defense of her master's thesis in hydrogeology and to fulfill a decades-long dream of mine to stand on the Khumbu Glacier at Everest Base Camp, that tumultuous river of ice I had repeatedly read about during my sedentary decades of armchair adventuring.

Without having received the gift of running four years earlier, and the improved health and fitness continual trail running imparted on our lives, that Himalayan trek would have remained an unfulfilled longing, played out in my imagination on small local hills—never the super-sized in-your-face mountain reality it became. This was the gift a decent level of physical fitness gave us.

In many ways, Cindy and our outdoorsy daughter, Jeanette, the dancer-turned-hiker/runner, were partners in my running journey. Not partners in the big ultra-distances, but partners in the routine of participating in the fun local road races, 5 Peaks races, the occasional half-marathon, and of hiking and exercising regularly. Routine builds strength, and strength breeds confidence, and confidence gave the three of us the ability to say yes to going to Mount Everest Base Camp and falling in love with the family of Pemba Tenzing Sherpa (nephew of Tenzing Norgay, co-conqueror of Everest with Sir Edmund Hillary) and his wife Nema, our gracious, strong, and caring guides. The fitness we gained through running also kept us moving at an altitude of 18,000 feet, and above, when our bodies deteriorated at the extreme elevation and when hiking became shuffling. Endurance, more than anything else, got us to our destinations. I don't think Cindy and I would ever have had the courage to go on that adventure if we hadn't proven to ourselves that we had the strength to go reasonably far in the mountains behind our home.

———

The March 2016 ultra-races in Monument Valley Navajo Tribal Park, Arizona gave Cindy and me our first introduction to the Colorado Plateau, the large, geologically diverse and colour-infused high desert region of the US Southwest. In stark wilderness terrain, with special Navajo hosts, Cindy ran the 25K course around the famous mittens, and I took on the 50K. Vertically less challenging than the Squamish50K, the Monument Valley 50K substituted the hardships of windswept sand for "vert" and delivered trails through time-sculpted mesas and monolithic tinted towers that were, to me, living, ancient art. We ran around, on, and through a fractured, crumbling wonderland.

But an ultra after a three-week Everest trek after an ultra in a seven-month span was not an exercise regime I could sustain, and I sensed burnout coming in the peak weeks of my Monument Valley training. Despite the uplifting grandeur of the event, completing the distance tore me down. Once again, I left it all out on the course. There was no charge left in the battery to get me any farther than the finish line of my second 50K.

To facilitate recovery, I set a schedule that only included shorter local races—nothing more than 25 kilometres—for the remainder of 2016. I also carved my training down so that it would not exceed 50 kilometres per week. That would give me at least six months of recovery before I went snooping for my next 50K.

Business life injected itself into my decision to step back as well. As Edmonton's neighbourhoods expanded in the 2010 to 2015 boom years, opportunities arose to expand the Great Clips footprint in the city. Starting in 2010, our strategic plan had been to build two new salons per year, but in 2016 three new shopping centres reached completion simultaneously, and the possession dates on our leases—some signed years earlier—all tumbled out in quick succession. Our historic measured pace for expansion was abandoned in 2016 and replaced with a spring and summer sprint to construct our leasehold improvements, hire and train the staff, and get the salons open. With top-notch Regional Manager Sandy Dahlgren in place, we were confident that if I built the salons, she could staff them. A location in an older centre in Edmonton also became available, and we took it to keep the competition out. In Vancouver, a poorly timed shopping centre teardown forced an immediate relocation of our older downtown salon, so the work of deconstructing it and rebuilding it elsewhere piled on too.

Five builds in total, four grand openings, one closure, and one re-opening—2016 became my business ultra. It was an overwhelming increase in workload compared to previous years. During the fall of that hectic year, I often commented that I didn't think I could have handled it all if I hadn't honed my perseverance skills over the two sixteen-week training cycles for Squamish and Monument Valley. I needed every ounce of the mental stick-to-itiveness I'd cultivated while training to go far to make it through that season of building, managing, and marketing.

As spring became summer and business consumed my days, nights, and weekends, I decided that future races would not exceed 50 kilometres. Two ultras down, I sensed I'd hit my distance limit, both physically and in relation to how much training time I could devote to ultrarunning. And I was OK with that. An eight-to-ten-hour 50K was darned long. I honestly didn't think I had it in me to race longer distances at that point, let alone ever have the time to add the extended hours required to train for a 50-mile or 100K race. In 2016, I felt I'd reached my happy trail running top end.

That August, Cindy and I returned to the Squamish50 for our third straight year, as volunteers, not runners, course marshalling the SQ50-Mile on Saturday, and the 23K and 50K races on Sunday. That was the weekend of my infamous runner-past-cutoff-late-night "boardwalk place" walkout with Ann, whom I would meet again one year later while climbing DeBeck's Hill, on my own SQ50-Mile.

How I got to that 50-miler, after I'd pledged not to race farther than 50K, was the result of one day of procrastination. And it all set me on an unexpected course to go really far.

———

Our 2015 Himalaya adventure retained a strong hold on Cindy and me for a number of reasons. We fell in love with our guides, Pemba and Nema, their functional Buddhism that permeated every aspect of their interactions with us, the Sherpa people of the Khumbu Valley, and with our Nepalese Kathmandu agent Hari

Prasai and his family who took Jeanette into their household when she extended her personal explorations after our joint trek. We were also affected by setting foot on a fabled part of the world. *Being* in a place, on the ground, with the people, in their homes, was distinct for us from *visiting* a place as tourists. In the company of Hari, Pemba and Nema, we were able to *be* in Nepal. *Visiting* yielded comparisons. *Being* led to understanding.

So, when the tasks and pressures of business threatened to overtake me in the fall of 2016, Cindy orchestrated an escape between the opening of our fourth new salon and the height of construction on our fifth, by finding us spots on a 136-kilometre Patagonia O Circuit trek in southern Chile in late October. We prepared in a rush and headed to another fabled land that Cindy and I had been longing to see ever since we each read Charles Darwin's *The Voyage of the Beagle*.

As in Nepal, we became good friends with our guide, mountain climber Diego Aldrete, and we were awed by the rugged, yet polished glacial geology of the Torres del Paine region. The grassy meadows leading to camp Dickson, the Los Perros campsite sheltered from hurricane-strength winds behind rocky moraines, howling John Gardner Pass where rocks clattered in knock-you-over gusts, the expansive white-blue river of Grey Glacier's ice, and the iconic granite spires above the silty lake at Mirador las Torres. The majestic terrain offered more than a respite from the challenges of work, it inspired me to hope that I could once again get out in our local mountains in the coming year.

When our Patagonia trek was complete, we spent a day in gale-blasted Punta Arenas before our flight out. That day was also registration day for the 2017 Squamish50 races, and I had decided to run the SQ23 together with Cindy for a second time. The problem was that the hotel internet was flaky, and I wasn't as persistent as Cindy, who managed to register.

I'll do it after I fly home. No problem.

When we got home, the SQ23 was sold out. ... The SQ50K too. *Gulp.*

Seeing the remaining 50-mile slots disappearing and overtaken by a sudden fear of not running anything, I paid the entry fee for the following year's Squamish50-Mile race.

Five and a half years earlier, I had started running by accident. Now I was about to start my quest to go really long, because of negligence. A bit shocked by what I had just signed up for, I had no idea if I had a 50-mile in me or not.

———

My analysis of the dog-tired endings of my first two 50K ultramarathons concluded that my training plans were barely getting me there. Up to 2016, I had worried about injury and burnout when I put my weekly mileage targets together. I would have to be braver if I wanted to get through the SQ50-Mile. It wasn't an easy course with over 11,000 feet of elevation gain—the same gain Mount Everest climbers ascend from base camp to summit. I'd already run the last 50 kilometres of it in the SQ50K and got beat up pretty bad. That would only be exacerbated by tacking an extra 30 kilometres and two mountain climbs onto the front of the race.

After much research into running long at an older age, I knew I had to ramp up my mileage in early spring with a greater emphasis on rest periods during my concentrated sixteen-week plan. In May, I paced Cindy on her first full marathon at the BMO Vancouver Marathon. She did well, and it was a far more enjoyable outing than my icicle bonk back in 2014. Wiser about what our bodies required to go far, we both fuelled appropriately and were not famished at the finish line. Feeling good definitely added to the fun of capturing Cindy's first marathon together—a milestone achievement for her at age fifty-three.

Cindy's full marathon appeared on my calendar as just one of several 40-kilometre days during my training. Prior to signing up for the SQ50-Mile, I had only experienced two marathon-length training days—one in each of my 50K training blocks. Heading toward a 50-mile race, half-marathon and marathon days appeared regularly throughout my schedule. On two weekends I ran a marathon distance on Saturday and again on Sunday. 10Ks— those impossible distances never dreamed of prior to my groin injury—were sprinkled about as short recovery runs.

The excesses of training that became commonplace for me as an ultrarunner ceased to be relatable to most others. I either had to quietly accept the weirdness of that or, if I shared my exploits, risk being berated for being daft while receiving a stare of pitying incomprehension meant to underscore it. Maintaining silence with my many non-ultra friends and relatives was the best choice. It may even have turned me into a better listener, as I had little else to talk about beyond my two big-time consumers: the conversation taboos of business and running.

Next on our agenda, and perfectly placed in my 50-mile training regime, was an appealing destination race in Utah planned for June 17, 2017: the Bryce Canyon Ultras. I toed the start line of the 50K, Cindy the 25K. The Bryce Canyon race, with its red rock canyons and multi-coloured hoodoos, ended prematurely for me when I clawed my way out of the race to make it to a highway and be rescued by ambulance. Cindy, on the other hand, fought her way to her finish line like a champ and did not require rescuing! (Chapter 5, The Flaming DNF, awaits with detailed disclosure.) Apart from the significant ultrarunning and life lessons learned in that transformative event, what mattered most as I headed toward the Squamish50-Mile was that I got in about 39 training kilometres that day—acceptable—and managed to escape with my life— critical.

Two months later, following a brief recovery and one final

three-week block of peak training, came the Squamish50-Mile. I had put in the expanded miles. I had increased my climbing strength. And after casting off my Bryce Canyon DNF demon of self-doubt, as recounted in this book's prologue, I was happy.

Coming down off the first big climb up DeBeck's Hill, where I had just parted ways with Ann, the revenge runner who forgave me, I came upon a guy standing with his mountain bike on Jack's Trail leading to the second aid station. He cheered me loudly; I waved and carried on. I met him again at the next aid station, and the next, the whole way through. Clearly, he was pedalling around the side trails to cheer a runner who remained behind me. (Where he got, and when he got there that day was no small feat, either. He was one strong mountain biker.)

At the last aid station, there he was again. As I climbed past him on the hill to the water, watermelon, and chips, he laughed. "You've had the exact same smile on your face all day!"

Photos taken that day prove him right. My big, toothy smile lit up all the pictures. Happy as heck. I loved that day. I wasn't fast, finishing in over sixteen hours, less than an hour from race cutoff, but I was consistent, and I was strong to the end. Wolfing down my finish line burger, with a medal around my neck, I knew I had it in me to go farther. My legs were aching but not done. My training had taken me to the end and left me with fuel in the tank— and the ability to consume solid calories—something I couldn't do in the final 10 kilometres of my previous 50K races.

Procrastination in Punta Arenas had pushed me up to the next rung on the ultramarathon ladder and reaching the 50-mile bar gave me the hankering to pull myself up to 100K. That was how the running far drug worked. Had I been able to register for the SQ23 the previous November, I may never have chosen to go farther than 50K. It wasn't the "tick-off-the-box" attainment of the SQ50-Mile race medal that enticed me to venture beyond that newly established border. It was the *feel* of the hardship of

50 miles and the *thrill* of overcoming it that was the lure. After experiencing the fatigued joy of the SQ50-Mile race, I wanted to feel what the end of a 100K race was like. Covering the 50-mile distance had pushed my body into new territory. My body wanted more. And my mind too.

We can be so wrong about the limits we place on ourselves. I absolutely knew at the end of my smiling SQ50-Mile that I had a 100K in me. I knew I could have done it that night. I'd already been on my feet for sixteen hours. Another 20 kilometres would have taken me just four more. Getting braver with my training had yielded results and completely dismantled my belief that going 50 kilometres was my endurance ceiling.

Cindy and I ended a fantastic year on the run in Kanab, Utah, where we took part in the three-day, three race, Vacation Races Trailfest, October 5 to 7. The races that year were in Bryce Canyon, Zion, and on the north rim of the Grand Canyon. A highlight was running the final miles of the Bryce Canyon race I did not finish the previous June. Crossing that finish line with Cindy was especially sweet. No ambulance required.

———

Developments in my business life at the end of 2017 forewarned me that 2018 might not be the year for big training miles—an attempt at a 100K would have to wait.

New Year's 2018 crashed upon us with the soul-crushing DNF of our remote salon in Lloydminster, AB, which permanently closed at Christmas 2017 after only sixteen months of operations, due to lack of employees. Our management team out of Edmonton was valiant in their attempts to save it, but in the end, having no hands with scissors in them was the final cut. Signatories on a lease signed during the boom, we opened our Lloyd Great Clips in 2016 as the downturn began. Changing government ideologies, both provincially and federally in 2015, ensured that the Alberta boom/bust cycles came to an end. A future upturn would not come.

When long-term federal government assistance for displaced oil workers finally came to an end and the Alberta economy fully tanked, resource-based Lloydminster emptied out. The result was that no new businesses waited in the wings to snatch up our prime location in a stillborn shopping centre. We were tethered inextricably to the remaining years of payments on our five-year lease.

With that costly closure, my successful run of building and opening new Great Clips locations came to an end. My days of managing our Edmonton salons came to an end that year too, with the sale of half of our holdings in the city in March, and the sale of our remaining Edmonton salons in September. Selling was as complicated and time-consuming as building. So, as Mark and I extracted ourselves from Edmonton, I did with my running life what I'd done back in 2016: I shrunk it down to accommodate the expanding workload and maintain space for family and friends.

But what fun Cindy and I had with the local races that year.

I ran four of the five 5 Peaks Enduro races, varying in length from 10 to 15 kilometres, and Cindy ran the 5-to-7-kilometre sport courses. We cherished the monthly interactions with our fellow 5 Peaks participants and volunteers through the summer. The 5 Peaks BC race director at that time, my friend and mentor, and the co-owner of the Capra Trail & Mountain Running Store, "Lady-of-the-Trails" Solana Green, who I initially got to know during her *Beast Mode on the Run* blogging years, had built a marvellous and supportive trail community around those races. Cindy and I were always pained if Cindy's nursing shifts, or my work travel to Alberta, kept us from participating in any of our summertime race-of-the-month community outings.

I entered four of the Coast Mountain Trail Running (CMTR) races that year as well. The CMTR races were more aggressive. A 35K, like the aptly named Survival of the Fittest, which ran in

Squamish in May, essentially played out like a 50K in terms of the effort required to tackle the elevation and technical terrain. The late July Buckin' Hell 30K race once again handed me my ass with a ton of vertical metres and some of the most technical terrain available on Vancouver's North Shore Mountains, including tangles of roots and fallen trees embedded in steep mud. Added to that *fun* was the fact that Squamish50 race directors Gary and Geoff also owned and directed the CMTR races. As a result, the environment we loved so much in Squamish each August was available to be experienced elsewhere in the Coastal Mountains surrounding Vancouver. The CMTR runners I spent trail time with, and the volunteers who so generously crewed the aid stations and helped with hydration, fuelling, and gear adjustments, inspired me to work harder. A day of racing at one of Gary and Geoff's events might tear me down physically, but the lift the human interactions gave my soul always left me higher in the end.

The previous November, I had not procrastinated on Squamish50 registration day and got a spot in the August 2018 SQ23. Why the shortest race? Because I loved what that race meant to Cindy and me, and I loved the people at that race. I also believed I could get faster at it. Lucky for me, I bumped into Solana in the starting corral, and we ran the course together in a time of 3:37:16. A thirty-two-minute improvement over my first effort back in 2014. Solana pulled me along. With encouragement, the old dog got a wee bit faster. And speaking of old dogs, our golden retriever, Kahlua, interrupted the SQ23 awards ceremony when I released her to greet Cindy on her final metres to the finish. Flipping around Cindy like a fish, Kahlua lost her mind in a frenzy of seal barks that stopped the whole show in its tracks. Since that day, numerous people have paused to ask us, "Was it your dog that derailed the medal presentation?"

Cindy and I kicked off the 2018 season by running the Antelope Canyon 25K in Page, Arizona together, and I concluded the year with a solo effort at the WAM 25K outside of Whistler, BC in late September. I took care of my body in 2018 by running shorter training distances less often, mostly as an adjustment to work commitments. But regardless of what drove the reduced mileage, the break my body took from running paid off. I wasn't exhausted when 2019 rolled around. I was ready.

CHAPTER 3

Going Farther

2019 would be the year I trained for my first 100K—twice.

Back in 2017, after I finished the Squamish50-Mile with gas left in the tank, I went hunting for my first 100K target and set my sights on the 2019 River Valley Revenge 100K in Edmonton. The race would finish on Father's Day and Jeanette and Cindy would work as my crew, appearing at the right moments throughout the race where they would assist me with hydration, fuel, and gear. With Jeanette living in Edmonton, plus the opportunity for me to catch up with business friends I hadn't seen since we sold our salons there the year before, the whole thing seemed like the perfect plan.

A few springtime races fit nicely into the training schedule for River Valley. One of them was in Moab, Utah, in March. We drove down for the Behind the Rocks Ultra races, where I ran the 30K, and Cindy ran the 10-Mile. The region surrounding Moab astounded us. Arches National Park. Canyonlands National Park. Numerous other areas brimming with geological wonders to be explored by foot, bike, and Jeep. To us, Moab felt like the Squamish of the Colorado Plateau—another town "wired for adventure."

In April, I took on the historic Diez Vistas 50K in the Belcarra Regional Park and Buntzen Lake Recreation Area, BC. Twenty-one kilometres into the race, I assessed the weather incorrectly, didn't layer up and had a hypothermic DNF at the 37-kilometre aid station. On the drive home, the shakes had me bouncing so hard I was worried that I'd goose the accelerator or slam on the brakes. I saw my hands on the steering wheel, but I couldn't feel their grip on it. Bad gear choice. Scary results.

A month later, with my confidence shaken by the freezing DNF and any belief that my training for the DV50K had been adequate, erased, I tackled a hilly 50-kilometre training run and knocked it out in 6:53:26, cutting more than an hour off my anticipated time. That one fast day, right on the heels of my frozen fail, reset my confidence. In my biggest training cycle to date, achieving that personal milestone was crucial for staying motivated. When it came to learning about the role my mind played in ultrarunning, especially as the distances increased, it felt like I was taking advanced courses at the School of Hard Knocks.

"A hilly 50-kilometre training run." What I once thought was my body's distance limit had become just another Saturday run. My training plan followed those 50-kilometre outings with a 20- to-25-kilometre run on Sunday, and sometimes a 40-kilometre. And then I did housework or worked in the yard afterward. I had indeed sailed beyond my old world's edge.

I was running up to 100 kilometres a week, averaging fifteen hours on my feet, and yet my body adapted. It was boggling to see those numbers on paper when I first researched and built my training plan. *Can I really do that?* But I had moved toward those big numbers gradually over six years, and the distance felt like a natural progression—as if my body was designed to do it.

One week later, on May 25, I pitched up for another gruelling CMTR 35K Survival of the Fittest and knocked thirty-seven minutes off my 2018 time. The result yielded a solid confidence boost on my last big distance before tapering for the River Valley Revenge in June. I was trained and ready for my first 100K ultra.

Three days later, on Tuesday, May 28, I ran a late afternoon 11-kilometre. A nice easy taper distance. At 8:30 that evening, with Cindy off at the hospital working a night shift at the ER, I was still a bit hungry, so I went to the kitchen to make some peanut-butter toast. I bent down to pull the toaster out of the cupboard, grabbed it, stood up, and my appendix ruptured. Zero warning. Knife-like pain.

I knew it was my appendix. The bounce-back pain when my finger was pressed on the site and quickly released was totally there. Cindy and I had learned about rebound tenderness from having to figure out when our three kids needed to fart, or needed surgery, or were just faking. That night, I did not have to fart. The internal firestorm was not fake.

But I had a 100K race coming up. *What to do?*

Google it.

Hmmm. Sometimes appendix pain can be temporary and with the proper meds, surgery can be postponed. *Thanks, Google. Good plan.*

I got myself into a position on the couch where the pain almost disappeared. I lay still for eleven hours. *Cindy will help me get the right meds and I'll be back in business. We'll save this race yet!*

When Cindy came through the front door, no doubt looking forward to climbing straight into bed after her twelve-hour shift, I got in a lot of trouble for thinking magically. I then had emergency surgery that lasted a long time because they had to scrape the literal crap out of me where my appendix had burst open, and junk poured into my abdomen. I kept Cindy up an additional eighteen hours—endurance training of a different sort for her.

The neat twist to the story was that the young surgeon who cleaned me out, and probably saved my life, was an adventure racer. He saw the pain I was in on the operating table, not from my damaged body, but from my wounded heart that was totally torn up about losing the chance to run my first 100K—a race Jeanette would crew—on Father's Day. He understood the drugged-up tears I leaked as I went under. He also said he would do everything in his power to cut me up in a way that would maximize my chance of a running recovery.

Our flights to Edmonton were already booked, so we went to visit Jeanette. I walked gingerly to the starting line of the River Valley Revenge 100K, where Cindy took a picture of despondent me with my useless race bib held over my punctured and sliced belly. I was overwhelmed by the feeling of having been robbed and beaten. So much effort had gone into getting prepared for that race. So many hours on the trail. All taken from me—a broken body left behind.

Then, what really got under my skin were the people who kept telling me that they had had their appendix out and were fine a few days later. I was not recovering like that. It caused me so much concern that I called the surgeon to see if I was a wimp. He laughed and said, "No, those people had their appendixes out *before* they burst." Mine burst and then festered because I believed The Google instead of calling an ambulance. He told me my recovery would be on the hellish end of things—deal with it.

Before I was able to walk down the street and back, I went looking for a replacement race. The only one that made any sense in the calendar year, and gave me any chance to get back into form, was the Javelina Jundred in October. It was sold out. Knowing it never hurts to ask, I sent an email to the race director, Jubilee Paige, inquiring if the race management company, Aravaipa, had any sob story openings. She promptly emailed back, acknowledged that I did indeed have a good sob story, told me to send in a waitlist entry, and stated that she'd do what she could.

A few weeks later, I was officially registered for the October Javelina Jundred 100K. God bless Jubilee. The only wrinkle in my new plan at that point: it felt like a rusty nail pierced my gut when I tried to run or roll over in bed. The pressure was on—I had just over four months to heal and be in 100K condition. Not that signing up was an easy decision—I agonized over dropping several hundred US dollars on Javelina and making it official— and the decision was made even more difficult because I dictated my own timeline, all the while knowing the trouble I was in. The tower of fitness I had built over four months and more than 1,000 training kilometres lay in ruins around the chair I had difficulty rising from. Could I get back on my feet and repeat each of those training steps all over again in the following sixteen weeks? The challenge was herculean. Never had I made a decision to restart a journey as daunting as 1,000 kilometres from a position where I literally could not move.

July 27, eight weeks after my gut blew up, I stood in the starting corral of the CMTR Buckin' Hell 30K adorned in my lucky green hiker shorts, favourite black running tank top, lucky hydration pack, lucky white cap ... every bit of charmed gear I could muster. After three full weeks of non-running recovery immediately following surgery, I had managed to walk 46 kilometres over six separate walks in week four. Setbacks followed with only 21 kilometres in week five, then 19 in week six. I finally ran my first 10K on July 16, seven weeks after the rupture, and that week concluded with 54 kilometres, the majority of them running. Then came Buckin' Hell. It was a big risk to set foot on that course, but I had to test myself. If I was going to make it to Javelina, my big mileage training had to get back on track that week.

Apart from how fine I might have appeared in all my lucky gear, I was very self-conscious about the way my belly looked. It was not its gently rounded potbelly self—it was lumpy. Visibly lumpy. It had those lumps because yards of intestine and other associated organs were not back in their right places yet after having been pushed this way and that while my adventure racer surgeon scraped me clean. Eight weeks out I was seriously concerned that I would have a misshapen belly forever.

Pain, not injury. That's what I told myself throughout Buckin' Hell. The part of me that hurt the most at the finish line was not my gut but my right arm. I had held it in an awkward position for the last few hours of challenging downhill so that the heel of my right palm could press on the surgery site and keep the jarring pain of the non-stop landings under control. My proudest moment came when I made the choice not to quit at the last aid station. I opted to endure the pain and persevere to the finish. It was the right choice; my tummy felt fine that evening. In the end, I was just dealing with temporary pain. I could carry on. My arm ached for days.

A week later, I was in the surgeon's office for a follow-up visit. He had a student doctor shadowing him that day and he asked if the student could conduct the interview. After verbally reviewing the surgery notes, which left him wide-eyed, the student asked a few general questions about how my stomach felt, how the incisions were healing, yada, yada, and then he asked me if I was able to walk around the block yet. I told him that I'd run the Buckin' Hell 30K mountain race the week before, and though it hurt quite a bit, I finished with time to spare and felt fine the next day. The student thought I was trying to be funny. Dr. Adventure Racer stepped in and, to the student's surprise, congratulated me. I congratulated him on the fine work he'd done to make my recovery possible. The meeting concluded with him assuring the student I was pursuing an atypical recovery. I owe that surgeon so much for not holding me back. He was excited to hear that I was gunning for the Javelina Jundred too. That was truly encouraging.

On August 18, less than three months post-surgery, I ran the Squamish23K in a time of 3:23:16, my fastest yet. The best memory of the day was that I was "that guy" on the last big climb, chug, chug, chugging past a slew of runners who didn't have enough in the tank to finish strong. Through trial and error, I had learned a lot about pace and fuelling over the years, and it paid off.

My last big mileage weekend, five weeks before the Javelina Jundred, coincided with the Golden Ultra Blood, Sweat, and Tears three-day stage race in Golden, BC. Day one, Blood, was a 5K straight-up ascent of Kicking Horse Mountain. The accomplishment of reaching the alpine, and the vivid rainbow that adorned the valley we rose from, were the rewards. Day two, Sweat, was a 60K full-on mountain ultra which included some of the most technical and exposed climbing on Mount 7 that I had ever experienced in a race environment. My gut didn't like it. Big pain at the main surgery site welled up on the descent from the summit. The rusty nail returned, and I knew I was flirting with injury.

At the first aid station on the way down, I asked for the crew chief, handed her my racing bib, and told her I had to pull out of the race. She locked eyes with me and asked if I was 100 percent certain that I wanted to drop. I gave her my brief medical history, she said I was crazy for being out there, recorded my number on her clipboard, called my name and number down to the race coordinator on her radio, and handed me back my bib as a memento. Done.

As an official DNF, I was rewarded with a bumpy ride down the mountain in a beat-up little pickup truck aggressively driven by a friendly and well-seasoned course manager who, from her gun-in-hand stories, still lived in the wild west, nearby.

Back at the spider-infested rental house Solana and several of her running friends shared with me (none had foreknowledge of the spiders), I had big-time DNF remorse and expressed interest in lacing up my runners for the Tears 22K the next morning. I learned later that had I not promised not to run on Sunday, my racing buddies, led by Solana, would have locked my runners in one of their cars.

They knew what I'd been through that summer, and they knew that my A-race was coming up in one month. They knew I needed to recover from my training and not push too far at the last moment. I started my taper a week early as a result: a good thing in the scheme of things. By that point, I had double trained for the Javelina Jundred. I was definitely ready—regardless of the Sweat DNF—and my tummy needed a rest. On Tears Sunday, I went out on the course and cheered instead.

The October 26/27, 2019 Javelina Jundred, Aravaipa's Halloween party in the desert, was a well-organized, entertainingly hosted, class act. Cindy had an absolute riot crewing in the tent city that ringed its way around the start/finish compound. There were interesting crews from around the world to interact with—fire dancers and endless Mardi Gras costumes. The dead ruled the night at every junction.

I finished the three desert loops that comprised my 100K race in a time of 18:11:11. It was one of those perfect race days with no horror stories, just happy memories of everything working right: from the gear Cindy helped me put together to cope with the heat, to Cindy's meticulous crew support at the start of each loop, to my surgery site and stomach being on point all day and me enjoying PB&J, pumpkin pie squares, and noodles at the amazing aid stations, to finishing the last loop with a guy named Chris who regaled me with race stories from around the world.

Up to that day, I had assumed that I wouldn't enjoy a looped race and that point-to-point races were the only way to go because everything would be new at every turn. Nope. Run in washing machine fashion, where each loop was travelled in the reverse direction of the previous loop, Javelina gave me the opportunity to meet and cheer on the winners and elite runners from both the 100-mile and 100K races numerous times. Furthermore, it afforded me continuous head-on "Hey runner! How are ya?" dialogue with racers of all sorts day and night. In terms of interesting interactions, it was the most social race I'd ever experienced. Repeatedly returning to Javelina HQ every 32 kilometres, where Cindy resided, and quickly figuring out the terrain on either side of the outlying aid stations, yielded advantages on the strategic side too. Hydration, fuelling, layering, gear, and heat management were all made easier by knowing what would be encountered where and when. For a strategist, the loops felt like a cheat.

Having executed a methodical and joyful race, I was very proud of the first 100K belt buckle I received at the post-midnight finish line of the Javelina Jundred—earned twice.

———

Two months prior to my Javelina Jundred finish, at an August race volunteer get-together, Race Director Gary Robbins challenged me to attempt the 2020 Squamish50/50—the holy grail of the SQ50 races—the 50-Mile on day one followed by the 50K on day two. Completing the back-to-back odyssey would give me all the finishes in the SQ50 inventory: 23K, 50K, 50-Mile, and 50/50.

"I'm almost sixty, Gary," I said with a tight-lipped, *you're joking* smirk.

"No. Seriously, Klassen, you can do this." He looked me right in the eye as he said it.

My grin disappeared. We talked some more. When I divulged that I was on my way to completing consecutive 100K training blocks, he pushed harder and wouldn't take no for an answer. I was surprised, flattered, dumbstruck, and terrified. Not once had I considered taking on the 50/50. It was just too hard. I was too old. But there was legendary ultrarunner Gary Robbins, pronouncing that he believed that little old me had the wherewithal to pull it off. Convicted by his firm statement of faith, I accepted his challenge. On the spot.

On the drive home, in panicky response to the startling magnitude of my quick commitment, I rationalized that I had already captured the first three SQ50 races, so earning the final double-header was a logical next step—setting aside the fact that I'd just leapt from impossible to logical in one conversation. Then I pushed my hasty justification one step further and mused: *At 130 kilometres over two days, the 50/50 was a logical next step to going 100 miles (160 kilometres).* For the next two months, I wrestled with the training requirements, extended running hours, necessary climb strength improvements, and sheer mental tenacity that taking on a 50/50 and then a 100-miler would require of me. *Was now the time to do this? Or more importantly, considering my age, was this my one chance to do it?*

The joy I took from my strategic and consistent performance at the Javelina Jundred in October was the confirmation that clinched it. I officially signed up for a two-race bib when the Squamish50 registration opened in early November. With a 50/50 race locked into my calendar, I then committed myself to going 100 miles on my own two feet before I reached the age of sixty.

The goal I labelled "100 by 60" had a straightforward plan—the 50/50 in August 2020; a 100-miler in the first half of 2021. The 100-miler I chose was part of the Antelope Canyon Ultras run in Page, Arizona. It was a race location Cindy and I were keen on returning to because the wilderness surrounding the south end of Lake Powell offered many slot canyons and different forms of colourful and irregularly-eroded landscapes that begged us to explore them.

Setting my sights on a 2021 100-miler had another benefit beyond getting us back to Page. If something messed up along the way (and my history revealed that things could mess up), the 100-mile 2021 target would give me one year of grace to make a second attempt before I clicked over the sixty-year mark in July 2022.

As I looked ahead to the 50/50 and the 100-miler, I was unsure which held greater emotional importance to me. The 100-mile race ranked highest as the top distance target, but the 50/50, with its brutal course layout, challenging elevation gain/loss, and dreaded Sunday morning restart, scared me more, even though it was 30 kilometres shorter overall. More so, deep in my heart, I coveted the cap the 50/50 finishers received. With all of the August history the Squamish event weekend held for Cindy and me, and because it was the biggest trail race in Squamish—our favourite place—I wanted to own it. In my mind, capturing the 50/50 on the way to a 100-miler would be like adding the mythic *nitro to the fuel tank* in terms of my confidence and motivation. I was planning on getting a resounding boost toward my grandiose 100-mile goal by sporting a blue 2020 Squamish50/50 finisher's cap.

———

At fifty-seven and a half years old, I started the 2020 running year with the CMTR Run Ridge Run 25K race on a rainy Saturday in February. As the mountain mists swirled around us at the finish line, who knew that microscopic viruses were drifting our way too and that all our well-laid plans were about to be derailed?

Run Ridge Run would be my last sanctioned race until 2022. My goal of running a 100-mile event by age sixty was in serious jeopardy right off the starting line.

By March 18, our Great Clips salons were shuttered. I found myself tied to my desk, trying each day to sort out the ever-changing health authority guidelines we'd need to implement to reopen. Then came the mad scramble for PPE and hand sanitizer. April and May 2020 would go down as some of the busiest working months of my life—and we were closed.

I had no time to run. I had no urge to run. In the early months of the pandemic, with the service industry closed tight, we were consumed by the potential death of our business and our future. Cindy's high acuity training put her on the extreme front line with the intubation teams in the ER—fully masked and gowned and in a continual state of readiness. My running calendar/journal has one purposely misspelled word scrawled across the boxed days of April, May, and June 2020: COVOID—the lost months.

5 Peaks offered a virtual race series that summer and fall, as did CMTR. Smart on their part. Good to have on my part once I

got moving again in July. Little race projects to sign up for on-line, and then execute in my running bubble of one. Like all Ca-nadian trail races, the Squamish50 was cancelled. My blue 2020 Squamish50/50 finisher's cap flew off into the void—insignificant when compared to the lost lives Cindy dealt with, or the failing businesses others struggled with. There's no need to elaborate on how all the disappointments took their toll. There isn't a single reader of this book who wasn't there. Has there ever been a more broadly shared joint experience of loss—from the trivial to the tragic?

Like everyone else in the business world, Mark, Sam, and I muddled our way through that disastrous spring and summer of closures and restrictions. On the family side, the kids and I offered support to Cindy, the swamped ER nurse, as best we could. As August rolled around and we began to fall in with the rhythm of the restrictions, the need to fill the void of all the lost race chal-lenges finally surfaced. I came up with the idea of summiting a local mountain, something I'd never done before. In the midst of the pandemic, with a business that was losing money every day, I needed something to win at, and climbing to the top of a mountain seemed like a way to fulfill that need.

I contacted a running friend, Jen Barsky, whom I'd first met, along with her partner Derek, when we shared the spider-filled rental house at the Golden Ultra, and we agreed not to be Covid-scared of each other on the trail. Neither of us had ever climbed to the summit of a named mountain before. We agreed it was a good pandemic challenge.

On August 14, 2020, we hiked our way up Mount Harvey, above Lions Bay, BC, and scrambled the final rocky approach to its 1,652-metre peak, where we took in a panoramic view of island-speckled Howe Sound, the glistening Georgia Strait, and the countless rumpled mountains strewn out to the eastern hori-zon, extending north to south. We didn't dance like maniacs on the summit, but we should have. It felt like we'd risen above all the pandemic worries below. It was still. It was blue. Everywhere. The clear sky, the ocean, the bluish haze misting about the distant mountains. Jen and I kept laughing, "It so blue up here!"

After months of losing, it was good for the soul, and the mind, to win at something.

In October, I was drawn into Jen's expanded running bubble, and we climbed through dazzling golden larches to summit Mount Frosty in Manning Park on the Canada/US border. The bubbly foursome of Jen Barsky, Jennie Woo, Didi Dufresne, and me became the Frosty Four that day. As we ran the long route down and out, our bubble bounced into another bubble led by our mutual 5 Peaks running acquaintance, Suzanne Pearce—also of the spider rental house. Just over a year later, I would burst Suzanne's bubble as part of my biggest running debacle to date. In November, I made a snowy solo ascent of Alouette Mountain in Golden Ears Provincial Park. That might not have been my smartest move of the season, but it was breathtaking up there. And I didn't disappear, even though I did almost slip off an ice-covered bridge previously knocked askew by a fallen tree.

All those mountains were walkups with comfortable scrambles. Strong hikers did them all the time. But the ease of their ascents didn't minimize their importance to me. I climbed mountains to fight my business fears, the social isolation, and the feeling that the pandemic was pinning all of us to the ground. Summits replaced races in the mental rewards category.

———

On January 1, 2021, I posted the following on Instagram: "100 miles by 60 years. In exactly 18 months, on July 1, 2022, I will turn 60. Between now and then, my goal is to complete the August 14/15, 2021 SQ50/50, followed by my first 100-miler in March 2022."

I put it out there, something I'd never done before. Until that post, I announced race results after the fact. That way, I could make the DNFs a little less conspicuous. But I knew deep down those 100 miles were going to take more effort and focus than I had yet dedicated to my running projects. My IG gang was small, just some running friends and a few family members who understood what I was up to. After twenty-eight likes, I had a smattering of people on board who would hold me accountable.

A few weeks later, I also put it out there that I was adding speed work to my training. A few days after that, I didn't post that my right foot and ankle fell apart almost immediately with the pounding I gave them down at the track. My first setback.

Next, Cindy and I found ourselves analyzing the pandemic housing bubble, and in an opportunistic flash, we downsized from our Greater Vancouver home of twenty-nine years and moved permanently to a condo in Squamish. My March/April/May running calendar filled with moving-related tasks, and those months became a void into which everything in life disappeared, apart from packing, cleaning, fixing, and hauling long-forgotten items stuffed in nooks and crannies to the secondhand store or the dump.

Tragically, Cindy's mom was diagnosed with pancreatic cancer in April, and we lost her in July. Another void was opened: a sorrowful one. The first half of 2021 brought life and death and change piled up as never before. So many thoughts of family, priorities, goals, and responsibilities stirred inside us during that burdensome season. Cindy was tireless in support of her mom and dad, as were many members of her family. We were especially proud of our adult children and their spouses for the laughter, love, and care they shared with their grandma during the final dice games, and then, too, when grandma could play their childhood games no more. We made it through, together.

Continued pandemic uncertainty during our difficult months pushed the Squamish50 race weekend from August to October.

My inability to train during the injury, move, and family moments was given a reprieve. I adjusted my plan and pushed ahead. To enter the forest to train was to enter into some peace.

A welcome and imaginative event took place on July 3: Jen Barsky's "50 Miles On My Favourite Trails" self-organized trail race. Disappointed by the postponement of what was to be her first 50-miler in the US, Jen organized her own event and built it around her much-loved backyard trails on Vancouver's North Shore. Brilliant.

I joined Frosty Four buddy Jennie to pace Jen through her final 40 kilometres, which concluded with a BBQ and pool party finish line at her parent's place. Best race finish line ever. Her partner Derek, kids, and extended family hosted the aid stations. They hauled lawn chairs, water, supplies, and treats into the woods to meet us. They spoiled us with sugar candies and hot noodles and cheered us on in the dark. Suzanne from 5 Peaks and Frosty Mountain, lugged ice up to the summit of our longest climb, where we gratefully pressed it to our bodies and shouted at the shock of it. The bright scorching day turned to pitch black night, and we—three small orbs of light in a row on mountain trails—carried on to a midnight finish.

In the lingo of the sport, Jen "got" her 50-miler. She earned it. She owned it the same way Aravaipa Race Director Jubilee had told me I owned my Javelina Jundred finish when she embraced me and said, "This finish is yours. No one will ever take it from you." Jen got her 50-miler, and the rest of us were treated to a spectacular day with special people. Jen's homemade race was a heart-warming highlight in a difficult year.

——

My upcoming Squamish50/50 would hand me more than 19,000 feet of vertical gain over its 130-kilometre two days. Climb training became essential that summer. I incorporated an adventure theme into my plans that flowed from my pandemic climbs of 2020. Alpine training days yielded four new summits in August and three in September: Water Sprite, Seed Peak, Skyline Ridge, Little Diamond Head, Blanca Peak, Tricouni Peak, and Brohm Ridge. Each was a full day adventure and only one was solo.

Solana from Capra guided on four, and I discovered why she was such an alpine addict as I, too, thrilled to the natural highs our local big rock offered. Climb training to alpine meadows, with scrambles to treeless summits above, built leg strength and endurance. Navigation on exposed faces, where I was always in learning mode, took me well beyond my boundaries. Each outing built my confidence and stretched my abilities.

Don't quit. Focus. One movement at a time. Lean into the rock. Trust. As a fifty-nine-year-old, I was challenged not just by the complexities of moving up and down the rock faces, but by the inner voice of doubt that questioned why I would do such a thing at that point in my life. *Was this a younger man's game? Was I being foolish? What was pulling me up to these exotic and dangerous places?* Of my sixty-plus hours of run training per month, I dedicated around twenty to the alpine that summer. Mountain scrambles offered a good break from continual running, broadened my rock-related skills, and enhanced my belief in what I was capable of.

By September, the year had played out as one of life-altering homestead change and family grief, with occasional moments of calm, and bright moments of elevated alpine joy. My plan was to build on the summer's trail and alpine accomplishments, capture my long-desired 50/50 finisher's cap in October, and translate that achievement into my first 100-miler in the new year at the Antelope Canyon Ultras. It had been a rough year, but things felt like they were coming together to achieve my publicly announced goal of "100 by 60."

———

Nineteenth century Prussian Field Marshal Helmuth von Moltke said, "No plan survives contact with the enemy." On the weekend of October 16/17, 2021, my detailed Squamish50/50 race plan met an enemy called an atmospheric river (formerly known as a Pineapple Express on the BC West Coast). The moisture carried our way from Hawaiian waters that weekend arrived with invasive force. Trails became streams that kept racers in ankle-deep ice water for kilometres at a time. Halfway into day one's 50-miler, I helped a runner who had fallen and been completely submerged in a creek crossing where I'd never seen a creek before. Her teeth actually chattered. All the race cancellations during the pandemic were bad. That first race back was atrocious.

In our tarp-bedecked Jeep, Cindy and Jeanette braved the elements as course marshals in a remote location just beyond the midway point of the race.

"How are you doing?" Cindy called out through the raging downpour as I approached.

"Good," I said without conviction, and pressed on.

I DNF'd two-thirds of the way through the race at the Quest aid station in a bloody awful way. My crew boss, Suzanne, did everything in her power to keep me going, but a serious clothing malfunction was injuring me with every step. I had sensed the onset of a chafing problem when I passed Cindy earlier, but once again, magical thinking and an eye on the target rather than my current issues kept me from letting her investigate my pain early enough to potentially fix it. At Quest, in a dry restroom, I disrobed and saw raw flesh where I should have seen skin. It was inarguably evident that I had been stricken with wounds unfixable in minutes, let alone days. Standing naked on the cold tile floor, looking down at the damage I couldn't ignore anymore, I was forced to pull the plug on my well-laid plans.

I felt complete and utter remorse for letting myself, Suzanne, and the crew down. I *looked* strong when I pulled out of that race. I felt strong. I was bearing up well under the extreme weather conditions, apart from one fatal error in gear choice. It was an insufferable DNF, and I robbed the race from myself, and my dedicated crew boss, who had made a big sacrifice to give a weekend to a runner in a downpour with no anticipated reward apart from seeing him drag his ass across two consecutive muddy finish lines. I didn't even manage one.

In the days that followed, when I could only wear loose sweatpants, and definitely not underwear, my confidence in my ability to achieve my "100 by 60" goal wilted. *How was I going to deliver a 100-miler after a mess like that?* The boost I planned to receive from bagging a 50/50 finisher cap became a deflation when I cowboy-walked off the course, injured by a bad decision.

———

Thwarted. That word singularly defined the end of 2021 and the beginning of 2022. My Squamish50/50 was thwarted. The upsurge of the Omicron variant thwarted our Great Clips business for the second consecutive Christmas as customers, who had slowly started to return, once again shied away from anyone who might touch them. It snowed in Squamish on Boxing Day, and the snow stuck around in the form of nasty trail ice for the next six weeks. An early January ice and windstorm made navigating the trails feel like I was a bug in a game of Pick-Up Sticks. Good strong trail running was totally thwarted, and therefore, training was thwarted. I finally got Covid. Cindy finally got Covid. More pandemic uncertainties around international travel, the inability to manage the timing of PCR testing at remote destinations, and the renewed threat of mandatory quarantining caused the deferral of my Antelope Canyon 100-Mile to 2023. The race where I was to accomplish my big goal was lost for the year. At every turn, I felt thwarted.

With less than six months to go to my sixtieth birthday, my goal of "100 by 60" looked like a DNF for sure.

Thwarted.

CHAPTER 4

100 Miles of Friends

Just because the military acknowledges that most plans fail when enemy contact is made doesn't mean the military stops planning. Why? Because the very act of making the first plan teaches leaders to assess their situation and use their planning tools to create new plans on the fly. What becomes critical is the speed at which leaders make their adjustments on the move. Plan. Contact the enemy. Re-evaluate. Plan again. Contact. Adjust. Plan again. And again, and again, until victory is achieved.

The 2022 pandemic deferral of Antelope Canyon shot my March 100-mile goal race out from under me. Snow, ice storms, and Covid riddled my January running mileage with holes and left my training plan in tatters. But I was done with being thwarted. There were five months left before my July 1st birthday, and I was determined to achieve my publicly stated "100 by 60." So I looked back at 2021, a tough year of enemy contacts, and pulled out something special: Jen's homemade 50-mile run.

I pivoted on that.

With the chafing sting of my recently lost Squamish50/50 finish still afflicting my confidence, I put a call out to my running friends: Who would like to pace and crew me on a homemade 100-miler in April? I got a rousing response, including crew boss Suzanne (thank heavens for *her* show of confidence). By making it an event, and by gaining commitments from friends to participate, I carved my timeline in stone—exactly what signing up for another race would have done. The deadline gave purpose, and having assured myself that my training had to arrive at a firm endpoint, with no room to waver, I set to work making plans to pull off a Jen-inspired HomeRun100.

I stacked my crew and pacer team—no doubt about it. I surrounded myself with the strongest group I could—because I knew the one enemy most capable of thwarting the completion of my 100-mile goal was me, and I needed a team that could adjust to broken plans on the fly and push me past my failings.

———

It snowed and rained through February as my training miles grew beyond 100 slushy solo kilometres per week. It rained through March when my training miles peaked. April had a soggy start as I eased into my three-week taper. I trained to my Antelope Canyon plan and approached my HomeRun100 with as much gravity as if it were a fully sanctioned race. Peak weeks topped out at 130 kilometres. My two longest training runs were 57 and 60 kilometres, each followed by a 30-kilometre run the next day. I knew that younger and elite ultrarunners trained well beyond that mileage, but a decade of trail running through my fifties taught me that if my peak weekly mileage was similar to my race-day distance, I could get myself across the finish line before time expired.

I trained exclusively on trails and forest service roads—snow-covered, muddy, or other. I did not train on roads or sidewalks—not even if dry. They just beat up my old legs too much.

My crew spreadsheets were finalized and reviewed with Cindy and Suzanne. Aid station food and supplies were itemized. Gear options for morning, noon, night, and morning were laid out and tagged for which aid stations they would be at. Estimated times for my arrival at the aid stations were listed along with the names and cell numbers of the pacers who would pop in and out of the run at those stops. And multiple copies of my personal run plan, with its specific hydration and fuelling instructions for each section of the race, were tucked in the various hydration packs I would cycle through. I trusted Cindy and Suzanne implicitly to execute the crew plan. They worked well together and had fun doing it.

I was ready. I was in that pre-race mood where my taper had done what it was supposed to do: leave me champing at the bit to get out there and get it done. I wanted to move. I wanted to move for hours at a time. How long I could move was unknown. At Javelina, I moved for eighteen hours. My plan was to get my HomeRun100 done in thirty hours—a standard 100-mile finish cutoff, although many races extend a few hours beyond that if their terrain is difficult. Some 100-mile races have cutoffs of forty-eight hours! The difference between what I had done at Javelina and what I needed to do was vast—another twelve hours—but that was what the challenge was all about: entering an event where I would discover how much I could do. It was about breaching my previously established border and seeing how far beyond it I could go—the time had come to test myself against my HomeRun100 ultramarathon.

When it comes to ultramarathons, the 100-mile distance is iconic. The Western States Endurance Run is the race name that comes to mind for many ultrarunners when they are asked which race "got it all going" in North America. It's Western States—that *ultra-race* through the rugged wilds of California's Sierra Nevada Mountains that first set out to answer the question, "Could a horse go 100 miles over the mountains in twenty-four hours?" and then evolved into one of the world's premier ultrarunning events after Gordy Ainsleigh showed up on foot on August 3, 1974, and completed it in 23:42:20—under the race cutoff limit for the horses. That's where the 100-mile ultra was born. Earning a limited ticket to run Western States remains the right of passage for the sport's up-and-coming stars.

My HomeRun100 right of passage was a little tamer, but it

wasn't going to be a pony ride either. I did my best to lay out its hills and valleys to mimic the Antelope Canyon race it replaced, but it was hard to find trails around Squamish that didn't go up mountains far taller than anything encountered around Page. In the end, my HomeRun100 had 2,300 metres of elevation gain, 300 metres more than Antelope, and much less than the 5,500 metres Western States saddled its participants with. For a first 100-miler, it was more than a fair test. I knew that because more than a few runners and friends looked at the course I'd laid out and asked in dismay, "Why are you doing this?"

———

Saturday, April 23 dawned clear and bright. For the first time in months, I wasn't going to start a run in rain gear or have a rain shell ready in my pack. As I looked out the window and ate my pre-race cereal, the golden glow of the sun readying itself to rise over the mountains in the east expanded like a dome in the blue-black dawn sky. Scattered clouds, tangled up among the snow-covered peaks of the Tantalus Range to the west picked up the accents of the looming sunrise and brightened as if to cheer the start of the day. Squamish hadn't seen a glorious morning like that for weeks.

Geared up and almost ready to go, I tied my runners too tight, something I never did, and while loosening them to their usual relaxed snugness, I came to the realization that each footfall beyond my front door that day was a step on a quest to travel *100 miles* on my own two feet. The immensity of what lay ahead addled my brain as Cindy and I descended the stairs to the courtyard. Undiscovered country lay ahead. There was no turning back.

My first pacer, Alley Vause, met me in front of our condo at 6:55 a.m. Cindy took our photo. At 7 a.m. my HomeRun100 began.

Blonde, petite Alley, in bright blue runners, a warm vest, and headband to ward off the morning chill, was my number one choice to pace the first 10 kilometres. I wanted an hour of inspiration, and that's what she delivered.

A tiny bird of a friend, Alley's ability to inspire was disproportional to her size. Having borne the weight of a broken world on her small shoulders, as she and her husband Mike navigated the loss of their infant daughter, Charlotte, a few years prior, she possessed wisdom, and the ability to encourage with an economy of words.

An accomplished ultrarunner, Alley had intrigued me a few years earlier when she expressed her feelings after a difficult injury-related DNF at the Teanaway Country 100-Mile in Washington State. Her heartfelt loss in that instance had nothing to do with the finisher's buckle she failed to earn; instead, what she said she lost was the experience—the deep feeling—of pushing her mental and physical capabilities past their boundaries and through the ever-increasing levels of fatigue. The perseverance to motivate and drive a mind and body desperate to quit, the triumph of the will over the pain, and the exhausted euphoria of the completion of her journey through mountainous hell were the rewards she lost by not concluding her race.

I needed to hear Alley tell that story again in her mesmerizing Kiwi accent. I needed her to inspire me to fight for those things over the long distance and hours ahead of me.

We talked the whole way, inspiration and advice from Alley mixed in with all the catch-up questions we had for each other about our families. Many of my trail mates were the ages of our children, with Alley and her husband Mike aligned with our oldest daughter Krystina and her husband Joel. Trail talk often became family talk. Their stories about their kids got exchanged with my stories about our grandkids. A beautiful way to spend any run. A meaningful way to start a 100-miler.

Alley and I paced ourselves evenly on the riverbanks and dikes along the Squamish River. Running through the glacier-ground sand and scrubby thickets of Fisherman's Park, Alley gave me my mantra for the day: "He believed he could do it. And he did it."

The sun rose bright in the sky. My goal was to be at the Capra Trail & Mountain Running Store aid station at 8:15 a.m. Alley got me there at 8:14 a.m. A perfect start.

Suzanne recorded our arrival time on the crew sheet, and using my pace projections, she calculated when she and Cindy would need to be at the event's northernmost aid station location with our supply-laden Jeep. Cindy helped me exchange my light 10K hydration pack for a larger pack better suited to my upcoming 25-kilometre loop in the hills. One minute after arriving, it was time to go.

———

The first 10 kilometres complete, my HomeRun100 (160 kilometres total) became a series of alternating 25-kilometre loops, six in total, all pivoting on the Capra aid station, generously made available to us by owners Mike and Solana. Loop one took a northern track up into the Garibaldi Highlands and through the trails of Alice Lake Provincial Park.

My pacer was Jacquelyn Janzen, another young, blonde runner and family friend. Jacquelyn's colour choice for the morning was bright aqua—a light blue-green that made her striking blue eyes radiate. Jacquelyn wore bright aqua runners and a matching long-sleeve, which I felt paired nicely with my bright yellow long-sleeve running jacket with handy pockets on the back for my gloves. I'm quite certain others could have said our colours clashed and that we shouldn't have been seen together. I ceased arguing such fine details of fashion many years prior—because I always lost.

I chose Jacquelyn for the first climb loop because she was a pacing machine. On a practice run six weeks earlier, she and I nailed a consistently paced 25-kilometre that aligned exactly with my race-day plan. I also knew that pacing that loop, and then pacing the final loop of my 100-miler, was a 50-kilometre challenge Jacquelyn needed at the start of 2022. Like all of us, she had lived through two difficult pandemic years. Unlike most of us, she had witnessed the very worst of it as an ICU nurse. A broad spectrum of people suffered from the loss of community, the loss of income, the loss of events and goals, but few suffered the years-long hands-on experience of death—some of it tragically avoidable—the way our ICU angels did. At the beginning of 2022, Jacquelyn was suffering, and she needed to get back on the trail, in community, and achieve some success.

Jacquelyn arrived in Squamish ready to run, and together we knocked off the first 25-kilometre northern climb loop in a blur of fast hiking on the hills, easy-paced running on the rolling trails, much encouraging conversation, and in the end, arrival back at Capra at 11:44 a.m., sixteen minutes ahead of target time. In the parking lot, Cindy surprised us with little PB&J sandwiches cookie-cut into heart shapes. A loving way to eliminate the crusts that didn't go down well during the race!

———

In late November 2020, the Frosty Four running bubble had gone out to the Buntzen Lake Recreation Area to run the then-deserted CMTR Run Ridge Run course, my last official pre-pandemic race, in homage to our lost running season. The relentless rise-and-fall terrain on the back half of that run consumed my energy and had me dragging my feet up inclines I had speed-hiked with ease during the race only nine months prior. It was discouraging to acknowledge how much fitness I had lost since Covid arrived.

On the other hand, slight, toned, and dark-haired Jennie Woo stormed ahead on the final climbs and graciously held back with us on the descents, apparently no worse for wear. And then, after that hard outing with us, she went home with Didi for dinner only to return to the park to pace a friend through the night on that friend's homemade 100K run over much steeper terrain than we covered during the day. She easily logged 70 or more kilometres over those two runs. I saw Jennie in action again when we paced Jen on the final 40 kilometres of Jen's 50-mile, and when I entered the fray on that one, Jennie had already been pacing Jen for about 20 kilometres!

A nurse-practitioner and accomplished long-distance pacer, shy but to-the-point Jennie exemplified how unselfish and focused on listening a good pacer must be while still delivering strong direction and leadership on the trail. She really was the pacing package, and I learned something from her every time we were out. "You're moving with purpose. Keep it up!" was an encouragement Jennie used to great effect. I'm not sure why, but those words embodied so much meaning when I heard them, and they inspired me on a level deeper than a "You got this," or a "Good job, keep going." There was something in the word *purpose* that rang true for me.

For the first go-around on my HomeRun100's 25-kilometre southern loop, I chose Jennie as the runner to lead me through the purposeful execution of a three-minute run and two-minute walk pace; a staggered formula I used to maintain running strength over long periods of time. Jennie and I had a methodical and chatty loop, and I was heartily encouraged by it. When we got back to Capra at kilometre 60, crew boss Suzanne did the math and noted that Jennie consistently delivered a 6-kilometre-per-hour pace the whole way around—our exact plan.

With the help of my pacers, by 4:01 p.m., I had already delivered a 50K in 7:25:00—with some decent climbs in it—and more than a third of the 100-mile was in the bag. My race-day plan was bang on target. After donning compression socks, making a shoe change, and getting fuelled up, I felt strong and ready to head out once more. On the downside, Suzanne recorded that I spent twenty-two minutes at the Capra aid station—a good twelve minutes longer than I would have in a bustling race—so apparently, I was not quite ready enough. With too much early-in-the-game easy-going aid station chatter, I was potentially sabotaging my end result—a critical ultra-racing lesson.

———

After a 1-kilometre flat runup, the next 7 kilometres of my HomeRun100's 25-kilometre north loop were all climb. Sixty kilometres in, I knew this uphill section on loop three was going to be my first big test, and I was happy to have Jen and Didi as my pacers. Dressed alike with matching navy-blue hydration packs over black windbreakers, both had the habit of twisting their caps around in sporty back-catcher fashion to cover their shorter hairstyles—Jen's a dyed, dark auburn pixie, Didi's a brown, tight-cropped cut.

In a word, that loop was joyful. The three of us moved non-stop to the summit of the climb—an accomplishment that ranked as a highlight in all my races. Such a simple thing, to climb a hill, yet such a challenge when it was 60 kilometres into a running journey, and such a reward when it was achieved in a singular sustained push to the top with friends.

When it came to making conversation on those loops, I know we didn't talk specs and models of mountain bikes or gadgets. I was a lousy conversationalist about *things*. We didn't talk about other people much either. "He said this, and she said that," always felt gritty for me in short order. We talked about ideas because, like me, the people I gravitated toward were oriented that way too. The professions of my HomeRun100 pacers, in the order they had run with me thus far that day were: oncology nurse, ICU nurse, nurse practitioner, English department head, lawyer. And while I wish I could recall all the ideas and issues we talked about on those first loops, what I do recall is that Jen and Didi had me laughing, a lot.

At the north loop's 14-kilometre mark between the lakes, it was hard to say goodbye to Didi at the travelling aid station crewed by Cindy, Suzanne, and Jen's partner, Derek. The spirited company they offered to that point had been good for the soul. But a nagging rugby injury kept Didi from going farther, and I was grateful for the time and effort our wounded warrior devoted to getting me up the hills. Didi specifically rocked the longest and most uninteresting leg of the climb up a forest service road criss-crossed by spring runoff gullies. Staying about a metre in front of me, just a bit off to one side so we could easily talk, she moved at a steady speed without any breaks or significant variation. Jen and I fell in rhythm behind her and marched along like cyclists drafting the leader. I had made that climb many times in training. Alone, I would lose interest in it and my pace would falter. With Didi and Jen, I nailed it.

Cindy took a picture at that aid station of Suzanne in a grey rabbit onesie stuffing the pack on my back with extra clothing layers, or maybe gels, while I held a big piece of pizza. Behind Suzanne, Derek wrestled with a zipper on Jen's pack with a bag of gear dangling off one of his arms while Jen stuffed pizza in her mouth with a distant, focused, stare. It was a snapshot of a textbook ultra aid station. I looked at that picture afterwards, and a second one of me standing in the middle of the road with a big square of pumpkin pie in my hand, and Jen with her mouth crammed full again, and wondered, *What would a passerby have thought of our eight-minute flurry of clothing layer swap outs, rapid pack resupply, and pizza pie eating—all overseen by a rabbit?*

And how did I know our costumed parking lot fire drill lasted only eight minutes? Because Suzanne recorded it. That's crewing, too. Everything that happened was a lesson learned for the next race—as long as I had a way to remember it.

Faces filled and metabolisms refortified, Jen and I carried on with rejuvenated strides. Perked up by the solid calories, it was memorable to cross the 50-mile halfway mark with her—the friend whose homemade 50-mile ten months earlier had been the inspiration that brought this 100-mile gang together. We hit the 50-mile point in 12:37:00. My fastest 50 miles ever. The dream team was carrying me along and at that point I thought to myself, *Wow, if I keep up this pace, I could get close to a twenty-four hour 100-miler!*

———

Three weeks before my HomeRun100, I was cruising along on my standard 10-kilometre route when a bright-smiled, trim, athletic young woman running toward me called out, "Hey, are you Randy?" A half-second later, the fit, energetic, and friendly-voiced runner right behind her said, "Yeah, Dr. Dave's neighbour, Randy?"

Caught totally off-guard by these sparkling-eyed, effervescent strangers, I pulled to a stop and replied, "Yeah?" with a heavy emphasis on the question mark.

"And you're running a 100-miler, right?"

Embarrassed, because very few people knew what I was up to, and knowing I was no Michael Wardian, I replied with hesitant unease, "Yeah, but it's just a homemade thing I'm doing with a little group, and it's gonna be really slow."

"Great! Can we help?"

I can only imagine how flabbergasted I looked at their excited persistence, and I know I stumbled over my words for a bit as we continued an awkward exploratory conversation until I finally came to grips with the fact that these two ladies were genuinely interested in helping me, an old stranger, go 100 miles.

"Well," I finally said, "to be honest, I need a middle-of-the-night pacer because my buddy's wife just booked a quick trip to Mexico for them on the same weekend. So, I'm short a pacer for that loop. Are you up to pacing a slow 25 kilometres in the dark?"

The irony of my question was that the woman who became one of my loop four pacers was Kelly Young, who, five weeks after pacing me, would go on to run 137.5 continuous miles at the Capital Backyard Ultra and finish as the second-last female on the course—a twisted way of saying, in backyard ultra lingo, that she took second place! Her partner was Steph Corker, the accomplished professional Canadian triathlete, coach, consultant, and winner of the 2016 Ironman Canada amateur title. I would know nothing of their rock-solid endurance backgrounds until it all came to light during Kelly's loop. Yeah, Kelly could pace a slow 25-kilometre in the dark. *Duh.*

A week after snagging "ringer Kelly" as a fill-in pacer for my vacationing buddy, the second pacer for that loop let me know that the long-range forecast looked good for my race weekend and that if the weather did indeed break, he and his friend would head to the mountains to do a long-planned overnight ski tour traverse. So sorry, but priorities were priorities, and I totally understood. Within a day of his pullout, I came off the forest trail behind our condo and heard our young, sandy-haired neighbour, Karina Welsh, call down from her deck, "Hey, I saw that Solana posted on Capra that you're going to do a 100-miler!"

"Yeah," I sheepishly replied. "She wasn't supposed to put it out there. I kinda wanted to do it quietly . . . but you know Solana."

"Can I help?" Karina asked with raised eyebrows and a willing smile.

I couldn't help but laugh at my dumb luck. "Are you up to being a slow middle-of-the-night 25-kilometre pacer?" I had my doubts about Karina when I asked that. Professional, impeccably dressed at times, and lithe like a yoga aficionado—which she was—she struck me as more Pilates than pain cave.

"Sure!" she replied without hesitation. We made a few contact arrangements, and my loop four pacing issues were solved. My guy friends ditched me, the ladies stepped up. And for what would inevitably be a withering solo effort, I had done my best to surround myself with a steadfast team.

On the Saturday night of my HomeRun100, as Jen and I approached the Capra aid station at 8:56 p.m., four minutes ahead of target, I had no clue if Kelly or Karina would show up because at that point, I had no real clue who they were. And yet there they waited, excited and ready to go.

I spent twenty minutes at Capra that time around. My footwear remained the same, but I added a long-sleeve second layer under my yellow jacket and yanked on stretchy pants to keep my leg muscles warmer in the night. Running shorts went over my tights to give me pockets and a bit more warmth. Cindy reloaded my pack with the hourly calories I was scheduled to consume before I saw her and our supply Jeep again at the south loop's Hospital Hill aid station. Beyond Capra's glass storefront, the final hints of twilight were evaporating behind the mountains to the west.

I'm certain that during that stop someone must have asked me, "How are you feeling just over halfway in?" And I probably replied, "Feeling good," and that likely ended the conversation.

But if anyone had pressed me further by asking, "Feeling good relative to having spent a relaxing day strolling the waterfront and enjoying the beer gardens?" I would have replied, "No. Call an ambulance."

On the other hand, had they pressed me further by asking, "Feeling good relative to having just travelled 50 hilly miles in twelve and a half hours and knowing how close that was to being on pace to grab the brass ring of a twenty-four-hour 100-miler?" I would have energetically replied, "Hell yeah! I feel good!"

The suffering of that ultramarathon, like all ultras, found its context in my mind. And sitting atop a body that had already travelled 50 miles, my mind was choosing the "Hell, yeah, I'm good," option.

I recall being in fine mental form when we set out on loop four at 9:16 p.m., even though my body was in pain—a lot of it. My quads were stiff and sore, and the outsides of my calves held a dull ache. My feet felt tender. No blisters. Just beaten. A bucket of unhappy juice sloshed in my gut when I put calories in my mouth. I was in the process of going 100 miles and my body was pushing back. Getting to 50 miles (80 kilometres) hadn't been too bad, and with only 20 kilometres left before I made it beyond the farthest extent I had ever pushed myself—100 kilometres—I recall sensing the jittery anticipation of new territory ahead and wondering if all those aches and discomforts would spiral. I remember consciously deciding to take my mind off that thought, too.

"OK," I said to Kelly and Karina after we got through the short section of sidewalks and commercial back lanes that led to the trails of the south loop. "I planned about four-and-a-half hours for this loop, so we're going to have a lot of time together, and none of us know each other, so I want to hear life stories. Who's going to start?"

An intimacy swaddled our little group as we tromped through the nighttime forest. Our world became only that which was lit by our headlamps. Conversation came easy in the privacy of our shrunken reality. Our small globe of travelling light in the inky black of the woods was a safe place. Looking back, I can't recall who kicked off the storytelling, but what a hoot we had pushing each other for more details, laughing, being surprised, congratulating, sympathizing, encouraging, and stopping together on a mountainside boardwalk to take in the wonder of the Stawamus Chief's dimly lit stone cliffs beside glistening Howe Sound from a perspective few ever see in the dead of night.

Along the way, Karina told the riveting tale of having recently concussed herself on a long run in Ontario. Dazed and bloodied, she sought help from an unknown cottager. Through her stories, I learned that she was a distance runner, and a strong one. I was touched that her volunteering for this loop was a turning point in her recovery. She was helping me, and Kelly and I were helping her, too.

Kelly held me spellbound with her tales of growing up in a large family, pursuing sports to the elite level, and breaking away from the expected norms to live the nomad life in a van and pursue her passions. She was so off-leash to me and so endearing. Both became my friends in one long, dark loop around Squamish, the unexpected blessing of having two other friends pull out, and two strangers fill their places. Yet again, I was hanging out with trail mates the same ages as my kids.

I specifically recall how funny the two of them found the full name of the event they were participating in: HomeRun100, Captain Muffin Top and the Merry Dumplings. By the time we got to discussing the origins (Suzanne being responsible for the silly bits that reflected the team's corporate pride in being curvy athletes), I had become aware of Kelly's stature in the professional running world, and I breathed a sigh of relief that she saw the humour in it and didn't think the rest of us too juvenile for including her and Karina among the merry dumplings!

Kelly and Karina took me across the 100K mark in a time of 16:48:00, another personal best for me. I was moving well with 60 kilometres to go. We talked and laughed the hours away. The night was calm and crisp, and the forest, Stawamus River, downtown waterfront, and estuary were all spectacular post-midnight.

It was an empowering, victorious loop, full of humour and fresh stories of trials and errors, of broken relationships and love found, of minds changed and beliefs wrestled with, and two good screams when an unseen creature cannonballed into a pond with a sudden and resounding *sploosh* metres away from us in the pitch black of the Mamquam River flood zone. We pulled up to Capra at 2:01 a.m., one minute off schedule.

———

Once inside Capra, Kelly did the right thing and threw me under the bus.

"He's way behind on his calories," she declared to Cindy and Suzanne. "Didn't eat on schedule. We tried, but he kept saying he wasn't hungry and that he would focus on drinking his Tailwind."

Cindy and Suzanne rummaged through my gear, looking for wrappers. Their faces darkened.

"You really *weren't* eating, were you?" Suzanne curtly flipped a few crumpled wrappers from my vest pouches onto the Capra reception desk in a way that emphasized there were way too few.

Cindy waggled one of my 600-millilitre soft flasks in the air. It gurgled loudly with too much Tailwind in it. "Didn't drink your calories, either," she said with sharp disappointment.

"We kept telling him," Kelly and Karina chimed in unison, a ring of accusation in their voices.

I could sense they were both miffed with me. I had to admit, they had done their best to keep my calorie intake on track while I faked them out by pretending to open new fuel, when in fact, I was sneakily recycling unfinished business, happy to let the up-beat nature of our loop keep my two new friends from harping on me about calories as inevitable ultra-nausea crept into my gut over our most recent 15 kilometres. Aware of the warning signs, I should have forced the calories in, but with the loop feeling so darned good with respect to everything but my gut, and being so pleased with my 100K time, it was easy to say to myself, *Don't worry about it, you can put the calories in on the next loop. You'll feel better then.* And that's exactly what I did. I fudged my calorie intake in the belief that I could catch up on the next loop.

The plan met the enemy, and the enemy, as predicted, was me.

I avoided the conversation the four then had about how I might have just pressed my own self-destruct button, and instead focused on pulling on a thicker pair of Drymax socks and a fresh pair of runners—my beloved recovery run, cushioned Altra Timps. *These will make me feel better.*

———

How does an ultrarunner fully convey their gratitude to their crew and pacers? Words of thanks get partway there. Tokens of appreciation add to it. But ultimately, crew and pacers are volunteers; they choose to do what they do. And when they do it well, all the runner can hope for is that their victory—be that a podium finish or tearful fight to beat the cutoff clock—is reward enough to fill the measure of thankfulness that the runner cannot entirely express.

So much of that gratitude relates to the end of the ultramarathon—when things get hard—when crew, pacers, and the runner truly come together. When crew and pacers pull out the stops to get the runner to the finish. When the runner digs deeper than ever before to not let the crew and pacers down.

Having let my crew down with an embarrassing, medical DNF at the Squamish50/50 six months earlier, the remainder of my HomeRun100 became a fight to make up for that loss by somehow finding a way to reward them for their unwavering support as I crashed in the middle of that night.

———

For the first half of loop five, Suzanne stepped out of her role as crew and onto the trail as a pacer, along with my Capra Trail Running Club buddy, Sachi. The timing couldn't have been better, even though Suzanne's placement in that slot was decided upon two months earlier when she said, "If I pace, too, I want a night loop." It's also interesting to note that Suzanne's dual role as crew and pacer was one hundred percent reflective of how I'd gotten to know her ten years earlier when Cindy and I entered the 5 Peaks racing community. On race days, Suzanne (a friend who was our age and had snowy hair like us!) was at the registration desk. Suzanne was at the kiosks. Suzanne was directing traffic. Suzanne was running in the race. Suzanne was taking the tents down. Suzanne was key to making things happen at those events; her spirit of volunteerism seemed unquenchable. And here she was, in the middle of the night, volunteering to keep me moving.

As we headed out from Capra, I was determined to do justice to Suzanne's commitment, and I vowed to be obedient to whatever she directed in terms of calories and hydration. She was, after all, a double-degreed nuclear and radiochemistry expert at the Kwantlen Polytechnic University, and therefore, way smarter than me. The problem was that I was spiralling downward fast, and my ability to keep that vow was about to sorely test both her intellect and her backbone.

Five kilometres into loop five, we faced the climb up the backside of Smoke Bluffs to the Summer's Eve Trail. In rapid and dramatic fashion, I had flipped from being upbeat and moving reasonably at Capra to sweating abnormally and trembling. I was nauseous, weak, lacking oxygen, and my vision was unfocused—wavering quickly from side to side. And I was farting. A lot. With Sachi right behind me.

If Suzanne was the unquenchable volunteer, broad-smiled and

charcoal-bearded Sachithra Jayawickrama was the unquenchable personality. Sachi made his way from Sri Lanka to Squamish via university studies on the US east coast, arriving in BC in the summer of 2021. A strong road runner, Sachi bought his first pair of trail runners from Capra shortly after his arrival, heard about the Saturday trail run club, showed up, and after spending a bit of trail time together, we became instant friends. It was refreshing to experience Sachi's newcomer's perspective of the West Coast mountain landscape, and I had the pleasure of introducing him to his first black bear on an early morning training run in the highlands.

With my eyes fixed on the trail we were scooting down, I heard Sachi call out behind me, "Whoa! Bear!" I looked up, and sure enough, there was a big black rounding the corner on the trail in front of me. I firmly told the bear to go up the hill. It did. Then off Sachi and I went. It was a total fluke that my firm instructions aligned with the bear's lackadaisical intent, but their coinciding outcomes kept Sachi and me giggling for a while. I was honoured that Sachi signed up to pace me on loop five, starting at 2:00 a.m., and little did he or I know when he committed to the time slot that he would end up seeing me, and aiding me, at my ultramarathon worst.

After an agonizing and slow climb up the steep Smoke Bluffs staircases, the Summer's Eve trail became a labyrinth, with my vision darting everywhere but where I wanted it to settle. The nausea was constant as Suzanne monitored my gel and Tailwind intake, making sure I was getting back on target with a minimum of 200 calories per hour. She accepted none of my complaints or excuses, and calorie by distasteful calorie, she worked to pull me up and out of the fuel deficiency pit I had dug for myself.

By the end of Summer's Eve Trail, beyond the twenty-hour mark, exhaustion draped over me like a shroud, continually slipping down my forehead to darken my eyes. I repeatedly fought to push it back up. I careened like a drunk on the descents to the river.

I was completely unable to focus. A few kilometres later, heading along the Stawamus River dike toward Cindy's travelling aid station up on Hospital Hill, I was physically and mentally tanking, and I knew that after leaving Cindy, I would still have a marathon to go to make 100 miles.

After twenty-one hours and 120 kilometres on my feet, the word *quit* entered my mind for the first time. A marathon to go was daunting. Twelve and a half kilometres after arriving victorious, though mildly nauseous, at Capra, I'd been knocked into a deep dark hole as my fuel deficit landed like a bomb on the proverbial 3 a.m. to 5 a.m. ultra-fatigue battleground.

All the literature on long-distance ultras talked about the probability of the pre-dawn collapse happening to a runner. But how was I to prepare for a physical collapse I had no personal precedent for? And was getting to the pain cave, and experiencing it, not part of the reason for going on that journey? Was I reaping the conflicted reward some of my young, strong running friends claimed they missed when they pounded out their first 100-milers in less than twenty-four hours and ended feeling fine? Was I, the older, less powerful one, an early recipient of the harrowing prize they knew they would have to go 200 or 250 miles to discover?

Braving the occasional eruption of my backside, Sachi stayed a step or two behind me, steadying me when I lurched too far off centre, all the while laughing and cheering me up—the unquenchable pacer. Suzanne kept an eye on her watch, telling me when to drink my Tailwind or have a gel. For those dark kilometres down by the Stawamus River, good decision-making was totally in the hands of my persistent pacers.

———

On Hospital Hill, I robotically approached Cindy's aid-station-in-a-Jeep. Once there, standing unsteadily in a seasick off kilter stupor, nothing in the food bins appealed to me. In fact, everything repulsed me, except for maybe the donuts and pickles. All the aid station calories I'd planned on, like cheese quesadillas, pumpkin pie, and PB&J—because they had worked in other races, at lesser distances—turned my stomach. Viewing the inedible buffet Cindy had prepared, through wavering tunnel vision, nauseous, with cramping legs, I could not fathom how I was going to cover all my remaining kilometres without physically crashing to the dirt, unable to carry on. Though I didn't vocalize it, for fear of acting on my own words if I uttered them, *I was done.*

Thankfully, my crew and pacers were not.

Jacquelyn had roused herself in the wee hours of the morning to spell off Suzanne for the second half of the loop, and together with Cindy and Sachi the four of them redrew my race plan while I sat numbly in a lawn chair, wondering if I could get up from it. My head spun.

From what I overheard, dazed and forlorn, I believe their rescue planning went something like this:

Runner can't focus and is falling over? Put poles in each of his hands instead of just the one he likes. Who needs to see straight in the dark anyway? Keep him moving. Wobbly vision is not a reason to quit; but it's apparently how Randy's body exhibits extreme exhaustion. Note that for his next 100-miler.

Runner is failing to take in the calories he planned on because he is retching out the gels and bars and doesn't want his favourite ripple chips anymore? Package up bits of donuts and the little pickles he's showing interest in and have pacers Jacquelyn and Sachi put a piece of one, or both, in his mouth every five minutes—whether he wants it or not. Get his stomach working again. Do not accept any of his excuses to not eat. He must turn his stomach back on.

And DO NOT let the runner manage his own intake of Tailwind. Make him show his pacers that he is emptying half of his

600-millilitre soft flask every thirty minutes. Get those calories and electrolytes into him. Force him to drink until he pees.

On Hospital Hill, on my own, I would have quit. With a team, with a dynamic plan, I hoisted myself up on my walking poles and forced myself to start moving forward.

As the journey restarted, my will to persist swayed and rolled like the cheap, poorly balanced canoes that scared me as a kid in the swells of windswept Redberry Lake at summer camp in Saskatchewan. That's where my mind went. I didn't hallucinate. Instead, some ruthless part of my mind hauled out old ugly memories of fear and sickness to burden me with.

Descending Hospital Hill, I leaned on the mantra Alley had given me, "He believed he could do it. And he did it," as much as I leaned on my walking poles.

———

My pacers executed the second half of loop five in textbook fashion: one step at a time ... plus a regular bite of donut or pickle. Sachi had a Ziplock bag of donut slices Cindy put together. Jacquelyn had the pickles. I specifically remember the care Sachi took to dig out each piece of donut (chocolate-covered Long John, with those crunchy little candy sprinkles), and I remember the look of concern in his eyes. Jacquelyn discarded sympathy and shifted into nurse mode, her critical leadership moment coming when we exited the estuary beside the railway tracks and stopped moving, with me bent over on my poles.

"Gels. Now!" she chirped and dug through the pouches on my pack for my emergency 300-calorie stash. "Eat them."

Sagging on my polls I gagged them down, amazed that they didn't shoot back up. It was all I could do to remain on my feet and not fall down and retch. Sachi stood at my side, his face sad, staring at the ground. I felt so bad for putting him through this awful trudge through the night. But dawn was beginning to light the mountaintops behind us.

"Let's go. One step. Then another one," Jacquelyn said after she took the sticky empties and bundled them back in my pouch.

One donut bite, one little pickle, one sip of Tailwind, one sip of water, one step at a time got us to the Mamquam River. I loved the trail along the riverbank down there. We were twenty-four hours into the journey, and the sun was rising as gloriously as it had the day before. Two beautiful days in a row—a complete rarity that winter and spring.

My stomach started turning for the better. The brightening sky lifted my mood. Finishing would be a product of my mind—my legs were long since done.

Jacquelyn and Sachi brought me back to Capra in better shape than when I left Cindy and Suzanne on Hospital Hill. But the crash had been ugly. I was fifty-six minutes behind target time.

———

In the downtime between sending us on our way at Hospital Hill and having the Capra aid station all prepared for our next passthrough, Suzanne asked Cindy a simple question: "What does Randy eat for breakfast?"

"Cheerios."

That little conversation had big consequences.

"Would you like a bowl of Cheerios?" Cindy asked when I arrived.

I immediately replied in the affirmative and at the mention of breakfast food my morning wakeup switch flicked on.

"Gotta poop first, though."

Another good thing in the scheme of things as it was evidence that my guts were doing more of what they should be doing and less of what had ailed me. I'm not sure that General Mills will ever adopt the marketing slogan, "Cheerios and a poop for the win!" but if they do, I want royalties.

There's a video of me sitting on a chair, rolling my concrete thighs with a scary-looking clamp contraption to loosen up the IT bands and hamstrings, and Suzanne spoon-feeding me Cheerios. That's what going far looks like: people doing strange things together with a purpose.

By the time I departed Capra, fourteen minutes after arriving, Cindy had been up for twenty-five hours, and she had yet to crew the final travelling aid station and get back to Capra and set up for the finish line party with Suzanne and a few others. I had been continually on the move, and so had she, and to a great extent, so had Suzanne and Jacquelyn. Never underestimate the effort and devotion of ultramarathon crew members. The hours they spend setting up, tearing down, driving, monitoring, problem-solving, and more, can equal that of the runner if they, like Cindy, don't check out of their own endurance event and take a nap. If a runner is not inspired to finish by the effort their crew puts into their success, then they're not paying attention.

————

I left Capra one last time in the company of Jen and Jacquelyn. Jen would end up with 50 kilometres on the weekend. Jacquelyn would put in 62.5 kilometres. Formidable commitments on both of their parts. How fortunate I was to have all these folks creating a human tailwind to help me achieve my dream.

By the time we reached the Smoke Bluffs staircases my vision had stabilized. Gels, donut slices, and pickles continued to go in. The only excessive hardship of the final loop was anything associated with going downhill—the pain in my feet and legs was all-encompassing; not one muscle was happy. But my legs never buckled. I just had to suck it up as pain, not injury.

I remember how fresh and spring-like our journey along the Stawamus River was that morning. I also remember how Jennie's encouragement to "move with purpose" was a central focus of mine through that whole section. Whenever I would slow down I would hear *Purpose, Purpose,* in my head and quicken my pace to get my footfalls back to a rhythm that I knew could move me consistently at 5 kilometres per hour.

I was pleased when Jennie surprised us and joined the pacing party at Hospital Hill for the final 12.5 kilometres. It was fun to listen to my three pacers talk—a mix of old friends and new friends with so much in common. Their conversations buoyed me.

I was aware too of how they all kept glancing at their watches. Jen finally named the elephant on the trail. "Can you run?"

They all knew my "A" goal was to finish my HomeRun100 in thirty hours or less and that my "B" goal was to just finish; there was no "C" goal. They also knew, once we were into the estuary, that the clock was ticking toward thirty hours and that the time to pick up the pace was right then or never. A fast hike would not get me an "A" finish.

By that point, I too had struggled through the math in my exhausted mind—and I had assessed my aching body. I made my decision: I would attain my "B" goal. After a few well-argued challenges, the team accepted my surrender to second best, and we carried on at our happy tempo, enjoying the ocean, river, and forest, and taking in the mountain scenery that surrounded us on every side. Over those last kilometres, my event became "100 Miles of Friends," and that's how I will always remember it.

With less than 200 metres to go to Capra, our little gang passed in front of the parking lot where a Squamish50 orientation run had been staged that morning. (Kelly Young ran more than 30 kilometres at that O-Run with only a few hours of sleep after parting ways with our group shortly after 2 a.m.) And who did Jen spot? Mr. SQ50 himself, Gary Robbins.

"Hey Gary!" she shouted. "Randy's finishing a 100-miler!"

Gary's "Heh, heh," laugh was loud. "No way," he called back in gleeful dismissiveness.

"No, he IS!" Jen and Jacquelyn yelled back.

"No way! ... Way to go, Klassen!" Gary raised his hands high and gave a few straight-armed bows in tribute.

That little exchange set the emotions of my finish in motion. Perhaps it was hearing and seeing Gary, an ultrarunner and champion I admired greatly, acknowledge what I'd done that got me choked up. Or perhaps, even then, in my final steps toward 100 miles, I felt the pang of my unfinished 50/50—the hometown race, and Gary's personal challenge to me, lost along the way.

I did run the final 30-or-so metres to the blue ribbon that Didi and Suzanne held across the base of the steps leading up to Capra. Cindy, the crew, pacers, and friends were there. Cake and goodies and beer. Cheers and a few tears. Many hugs, and Cindy's teary, proud smile. I floundered for words to express my thanks for all she'd done to get me to the finish.

The crew celebrated the bond forged in the shared struggle to get one runner all the way home. The party on Capra's front landing did not feel like my victory. We owned it together. Enveloped in shared joy, my strongest emotion was gratitude.

Capra team member Tiff Gibson shot a video and asked, "How do you feel, Randy?"

"I feel like I'm done," I replied, leaning forward on a walking pole, looking peaceful and relaxed. "And I'm happy to be done."

My friends kept offering me a camping chair to sit in, but I continued to walk and stand for a long while. Sitting felt like the signal of the end. It took time for me to accept that the journey was over.

Done. One word encompassed it all. The years of training and growth. The thirty hours, thirty-seven minutes of motion. The night's hardships. The crew's perseverance. The successful completion. All done.

He believed he could do it. And he did it.

"100 by 60." Life goal accomplished.

Falling Down

*When I was a kid, way back in the 70s,
I learned that I was never fully involved in
a sport if I wasn't falling down.*

CHAPTER 5

The Flaming DNF

I crested the race's high point at 9,100 feet of elevation in the early morning chill. The first 10 kilometres of the June 2017 Bryce Canyon 50K Ultra were under my belt, the biggest climb of the day was done. Then, with arms outspread in praise to the glory surrounding me, I loped in jubilant zig-zag fashion down the mountainside trail toward the Blue Fly aid station with a view of the rumpled Sunset Cliffs before me and a broad smile on my face. I heard laughter, looked over my shoulder, and saw another runner leaping down the path behind me, her arms spread like wings as well. Our hoots and shouts of joy echoed off the sunbaked terrain and gnarled trees.

We had shivered through a cold start that morning, typical of the high desert, even though the day before had reached searing highs. Rumours in the starting corral were that an abnormal number of 100-milers had dropped from the heat on the first day. To counter the morning cold, I began the day wearing an Under Armour HeatGear compression base layer under my usual running short sleeve. A perfectly legitimate gear choice, and the first hole in the hull of the ship that would sink that day.

Once we were through Blue Fly Aid, our clot of runners continued down the mountain as the temperature inched up, but being on the west side of the hill, we remained shielded from the mid-morning sun. Then came the second climb, a little more toilsome, followed by a brisk descent through tight woods toward Proctor Canyon. Nearing Proctor Aid, I came upon a US service member at a dry creek crossing. He picked his way across the stones on stiff legs and used his poles to hoist himself up the slick dusty bank on the other side.

"Go ahead," he nodded. His eyes were tired, his breaths long and drawn out. "I'm packing it in at Proctor." He was a 100-miler who had started the day before.

That rattled me. I stayed with him to talk awhile. Yesterday's heat had cooked him, and he hadn't recovered enough through the night to finish his last 29 kilometres. Ultras weren't his "usual thing," he'd noted, while keeping whatever usual extreme "thing" he did in his branch of service top secret. This event had looked beautiful and fun, so he signed up, but at that point he was done.

After we parted, a kilometre or two of winding trail brought me down to Proctor Aid. With each metre of elevation loss, the thickening air became more oppressive. The heat in that valley was like a tightening vice, and the exuberance I had felt earlier in the cool breeze of the high mountain shade gushed from me in the canyon's grip. Someone said it was 108 degrees Fahrenheit. There was no air movement. I rummaged through my drop bag, grabbed the fuel for my next leg, bars and beef jerky and gels, filled my hydration pack's water reservoir, and walked to the near-vertical trail that would get me up and out of the stone oven.

If I'd had a race-day running plan back in 2017—the importance of which I was about to learn—it would have told me to take off my Under Armour base layer, which I completely forgot I was wearing. I just wanted out of that valley and gave no thought to my gear.

I distinctly remember nine of us starting the climb out of Proctor Canyon. I know three of us arrived at the top together. We left the others at various points on the upward struggle, sitting, vomiting, or on their way back down. Those of us who made it in that group did so by going up a few metres at a time, then stopping. Up some more, stopping. I could see the confusion on my fellow runners' faces. They must have seen the fear on mine.

That climb was steep, but we were all trained to get up it at a strong hiking pace. In my trail running experience, the methodical steady push up an incline was often a welcome relief from the pounding of the flats and downhills. I often relaxed into the uphill sections. My heart rate would slow. My breathing would find a rhythm with my legs. Muscles would stretch out, and pain would ease. Though counterintuitive, an uphill for me was often a welcome obstacle. But on that sweltering day at Bryce, something was very wrong. That particular hill was *not* my friend.

I started to vomit 200 metres or so after the summit. I had not vomited since having the flu back at Christmas in 1996.

At first, I welcomed the upchucking as a potential solution. *Cool. I finally have an ultra puke story. You're not ultra-racing unless you're puking, right?*

I had great hope that a quick round of heaving would get whatever was making me feel so bad out so that I could continue with what had been, to that point, a good day. I remained on track for a strong finish time, despite the slow grind out of Proctor. I was thankful that the choking heat of the valley had lessened higher up.

It didn't take long for that hope to fragment and my thankfulness to evaporate. I could run down hills and shuffle the flats, but any movement on an upward slope triggered excessive vomiting: throat-tearing heaves that left my stomach muscles an aching block below my tender ribcage. The taste of a gel on my tongue produced a retch. A drop of water on my lips, a convulsive dry gulp.

Runners more accustomed to the heat passed me and offered remedies that only made me cringe. I asked a few of them where they were from. "Texas" and "Florida," I recall hearing.

"You're lucky," I said to one fellow from Texas who tried in vain to get me to eat some of his sugary dried fruit. "You're used to this heat."

"No, not heat like this," he replied. "This is a bad one."

Picking up my pace whenever the churn subsided, I started to pass runners in worse shape than me.

The food tent at Thunder Mountain Aid, 15 kilometres from the finish line, felt like a triage centre to me. I scrounged for ice and filled my reservoir in hopes of keeping my back cool. I dunked my head in the dipping tank and ended up on my butt on the ground, dizzy and fatigued. I thought about calling it quits, but the race volunteers already appeared overwhelmed with people seeking shelter in the tents and asking for rides out. The last thing I wanted was to get caught up in an endless extraction waiting game with a resolution out of my control.

I gagged my way up and out of the aid station with my sights set on what looked like a more wooded section ahead, desperate for some shaded relief. My base layer stayed on. My core temperature spiked higher and higher. Neither water nor fuel was getting past my lips.

After the big eastward turn in the course, just before the long final ascent up the winding, curling Thunder Mountain Trail—the crown jewel of the racecourse rimmed with red and gold limestone hoodoos—I hit the wall and could go no farther. I was at the junction where Cindy's half-marathon race joined the 50K for the shared 13 kilometres to the finish line. I had been in this place two days earlier when Cindy and I reconned the start of her course. I weighed my options: continue 13 kilometres uphill to the finish line and help, or escape 3 kilometres downhill to the Red Canyon highway where I could lie down on the road and be rescued.

At that moment, I could do neither, my exhaustion was just too overwhelming. I lay down beside the trail and fell asleep—or, more accurately, passed out.

My skin quivered across my body. I awoke covered with ants.

Not biting ants, thank heavens, just crawling ants by the hundreds. Scraping and scratching at them, I finally discovered my Under Armour base layer and ripped it off. I sat on a rock, topless, with my pack and shirts strewn about, red scratch marks on my overheated skin. To see me was to see my race: neatly put together in the early hours, now laid bare and in shambles.

A few runners straggled past. None of them looked well. None of them cared to glance at me. I couldn't imagine following them. Just the thought of moving upward sent waves of nausea through my gut. I made the decision to escape the race.

Less than 100 metres down the trail to Red Canyon, I met a young woman in white khaki shorts and a white broad-brimmed hat on her way up. She'd come looking for her boyfriend, who she felt should have finished his race already. Had I seen him? I think I managed to laugh at that. I told her that runners were suffering from the heat, and that maybe he'd dropped at an aid station and was waiting for a ride out. I told her what my plan was, and she wished me luck. I asked her to call the finish line to tell them I was leaving the race. She replied that she'd had no cell coverage since she left the highway. We parted, and I wondered if she, too, would meet the ants.

The 3 kilometres to the highway were a blur. I moved from shaded patch to shaded patch. I hallucinated. The slope was downhill, but the landscape kept rising in front of me, shimmering and wavering, like being on a sailboat in large rolling swells with no wind to propel me through them. I'd been on that sailboat, years before, crossing the Salish Sea's Straight of Georgia. I slowly rose and fell without getting any farther ahead, seasick and trapped in a blistering hot cage with no walls. I was sick many times as I stumbled forward. I remember when I first heard a car on the highway ahead and the hope the faint sound gave me. I vividly recall the moment two paramedics with massive backpacks came up the rolling trail toward me.

"Are you a runner from the race?" one paramedic called out.

I burst into tears, fell forward on my knees, and vomited to the point where I collapsed in the dirt. All I could do was apologize profusely.

The paramedic took off her pack and strapped it to the chest of her partner. Laden with IV bags and barely able to see over his new load, he then carried on up the trail toward the racecourse. She helped me up and walked me down to an ambulance waiting in the trailhead parking lot. Package delivered, she ran off up the trail again to assist her partner with the on-course rescues they must have administered for hours.

My arms were favourites on blood donation day back at college, when giving blood was a sure ticket out of a boring lecture and the guarantee of a cookie and a small glass of milk. Thick blue veins laced my wrists and the inside crooks of my elbows. But on barfing day at Bryce, my veins vanished, and after four or five unsuccessful tries to start my IV—some hooked up to fluid that painfully flowed into the tissues of my arms with rock-hard bulging results—the ambulance paramedic apologetically told me I would have to be transported to the hospital.

Envisioning our bank account disappearing faster than my veins, I pleaded with her to keep trying. She gave me a Powerade to chug down and went outside to instruct a group of military paramedics who had arrived while she'd been stabbing me. Through the open, rear doors of the ambulance, I watched a team of olive-drab medics, with impressive square black packs, head up the trail I'd stumbled down. I learned later that the woman in white who I'd met on the trail found cell coverage—and more racers in distress—and put out a call for help.

"Are you sure about this?" the paramedic asked as she pulled herself back up into the ambulance.

"Go for it."

I clenched my teeth, looked away, and she drilled for veins. The eighth borehole was the charm. Drip by drip, replacement fluids dilated my constricted circulatory system. With a look of miffed triumph, the paramedic announced that I had just set her all-time record for IV start failures—she celebrated by giving me a second Powerade. The combination of the replenishing liquids was soothing—like softly expanding back into shape after being sucked tight from the inside.

Over a ninety-minute period with the most caring and chatty paramedic, I went from vomiting in the dirt to expressing my desire to get back on the course to finish the race, having calculated that I still had the time to do it. Her vehement protests quickly dissuaded me, as did sober second thought, so I turned my focus to getting to the finish line by another route.

"Nope. Sorry," she said. "I can treat you for no charge on-the-spot, but if I transport you anywhere, I have to write it up, and you get a bill."

"And those guys out there?" I pointed to a few military medics who remained in their non-descript olive cube trucks.

"Nope. They can't move you either. You're not a patient anymore."

I collected my gear and thanked her for taking such good care of me.

How to get back?

I walked over to the medic's truck with two soldiers sitting inside. Before I reached them the fellow on the passenger side asked, "How are you holding up?"

"Good," I said and waved it off. As I did, I saw my forearm was dotted with little Band-Aids and bruises. I got a few steps closer. "Can you guys pick up hitchhikers?"

"Why?"

"I need to get to the race finish, and if you guys are heading that way anytime soon, well, I was just wondering … You don't charge hitchhikers for a lift, do you? I've got zero cash."

They looked at each other. The driver looked at his watch. "Huh," he said. "Seems we have to head in that direction in a minute or two." He raised his index finger up to adjust his glasses and purposefully dropped it forward in slow motion to point down the highway.

I started walking. When I heard their truck tires crunch at a slow roll along the highway shoulder behind me, I stuck out my thumb. And with that, I made it to the finish line.

Cindy, strong woman that she was, survived the blistering heat and finished her Bryce Canyon ordeal on her own two feet. Out of cell coverage much of the day, I had been worried sick that she was in trouble, too, but apparently not. Her finish line photo was one to be proud of!

Throughout that evening and night, Cindy's biggest concern for me was overhydration, the bounce-back problem of not recovering from heatstroke wisely. I made it through the night just fine. Then, after a rest day by the pool, we were back hiking the ghostly amphitheatre labyrinths of gargantuan, weathered and eroded hoodoos in Bryce Canyon National Park—one of the most unexpected landscapes we'd ever witnessed.

The Bryce Canyon 50K Ultra, 2017: best race I never finished.

———

Was it any wonder that sixty days later, at the start of my first Squamish50-Mile, I felt so unsure of myself? A physical collapse and DNF, regardless of extenuating circumstances, always added up to a complete mind-bender for me. I carried the weight of my June collapse along those striking Utah trails up DeBeck's Hill that August—the mental hurdle of feeling incapable being far taller than DeBeck's itself.

Was it any wonder that I felt for Ann, the runner at the SQ50-Mile who was avenging her DNF from the previous year? On so many levels, my time with her on that DeBeck's climb was serendipitous, and my joy throughout that race a dramatic departure from my hellish experience at Bryce.

Extreme emotions in an extreme sport, within a two-month span.

———

Inside that flaming DNF lay the key to not repeating the disaster.

In the weeks following my run-in with heatstroke, I went searching for the reasons behind my crash. Apart from knowing full well that I overheated my core by not removing my base layer, I needed to figure out how to acclimatize myself for races far from home with different weather conditions. Envisioning myself bundled in a parka on all my training runs with sweat overflowing my runners, I went looking for instructions on how to "train hot in a cold environment."

I learned that the reason things fell apart for me at Bryce Canyon was not that I wasn't acclimatized (I wasn't, and I never would be unless I moved to the desert for a few months before each future race). No, things fell apart because my body, trained in the cool environment of the Pacific Northwest, was shocked on my descent into Proctor Canyon, and it never recovered because I had no on-trail remedies to apply once the overheating started. Avoiding that "shock" was the key to racing in the desert again, which had little to do with acclimating.

So, how did I avoid the shock of a scorching race day in October, two years later, when I headed off to my 2019 Javelina Jundred, another notoriously oven-like desert race? I pre-heat-shocked myself enough times so that when race day arrived, my body shrugged it off and said, "Oh well, here he goes again," rather than freaking out and shutting down. I taught my body that sudden immersion in extreme heat was no big deal.

To achieve that in 2019, I stopped running outside in the rain when September settled in because rain and cold were two conditions I would not encounter in McDowell Mountain Regional Park outside of Fountain Hills, Arizona. Instead, I set up two portable heaters, dialled to 30 degrees Celsius, to blast me on our treadmill.

I remember one long run that took me the full length of *The Good, The Bad, And the Ugly*—over two-and-a-half hours frying on a treadmill. The sweat spray on the wall behind me after that long run was a downside; my ability to withstand the heat of race day, an upside. (And aren't the endless closeups in the standoff scene at the end of that movie awesome?)

I also heat-shocked my body at the local pool during the three-week taper prior to my race. Every second night I spent longer and longer stretches in the sauna, with the occasional trip into the steam room. I would do this for one hour a night. I wasn't a steam room guy, and the torrid squeeze of the blistering air in that tight room brought back memories of Proctor Canyon real quick. Through the heat training, I gained as much mentally as I gained physically. By pushing my times longer in both the sauna and steam room, I forced my body and mind to accept and deal with uncomfortable heat, something my research pointed toward.

Flying down to Phoenix, my body was prepared for the blast furnace of the desert. My mind too. At no time during my Javelina race did I become as overwhelmed by the heat as I did when I pushed my limits in the sauna and steam room—limits that were, in terms of absolute temperature, probably worse than the extreme heat that brought me down at Bryce. Never reaching my shock training extremes on Javelina race day made it feel like a breeze.

Could the heat at Javelina have exceeded my breaking point without that prep? Yes, I'm quite sure I would have experienced a repeat of the Bryce Canyon collapse if I hadn't put in the work to better prepare myself for the significant change in climate.

Javelina was roasting, but my body and mind were ready to handle the abrupt heat hit. In fact, the blistering desert sun almost felt welcome on race day.

———

As important as the weeks I spent stuck together with new friends in the fraternity of habitual sauna sweaters (there truly was a community that stuck together at the pool), were the adaptations I made to my running gear to cool my core rather than fry it.

First, I acquired the correct apparel for the heat. Some research and shopping put me in a short sleeve that had cooling properties when wet. A cap of similar material kept my head cool in the morning. I switched to a wide-brim Tilley-style hat for my afternoon under the blazing sun. Subsequently, in 2022, I discovered the Sun Runner Cap by Outdoor Research with a removable shroud that covers the ears and neck when cinched up. That became my hot-weather headgear of choice.

I purchased white reflective arm sleeves from an Arizona mountain bike shop, made of material with cooling properties as well. In the heat of the day, I stuffed the sleeves with ice at the aid stations, and though painful at first, I could get almost forty minutes of dampness out of each fill-up, and cool extremities felt so good while keeping me in the race.

Finally, Cindy made an ice collar that was easy to load and had a clip system so that I wouldn't be wrestling with tying and untying wet knots. The fabric she used for the collar retained the ice for long periods and gave me a steady drip of cool water down my back and chest that worked in tandem with the water-cooled short sleeve to keep my core temperature from getting out of control.

Had I been decked out with clothing and accessories that reduced my core temperature rather than elevated it at Bryce Canyon, and had my body and mind been ready for the searing shock of

Proctor Canyon, there's a high probability I would have crossed the Bryce Canyon 50K finish line back in June 2017. And there's the rub of lessons learned: they can give you a better future, but they can't salvage your broken past.

———

I often get emotional when I talk about Bryce Canyon 2017. Particularly my decision to venture off course to, literally, save myself. At a minimum, I imagine I'd be sharing a remote rescue and hospitalization story if I'd carried on up Thunder Mountain Trail.

What Bryce showed me, in stark play-by-play, was that when the worst was happening, I acted. I didn't wait for anyone to come to my rescue, I sought safety for myself. I found my way out. It also showed me that I didn't do it perfectly. I made the wrong decision to push beyond Thunder Mountain Aid—where I could have been extracted—and I made the right decision to self-rescue to Red Canyon—the harder alternative, but one that still saved the day.

Using that filter to look back at difficult times in my family life, and business life, I saw why I did some of the things I did; why I didn't stop moving when contact with the enemy was made; why I quickly assessed my situation, made the best decision I could, hit another roadblock, assessed again, failed, and kept going until I, or we, got out. Bryce gave me a filter through which I better understood myself.

As a result, Bryce revealed that I possessed a level of confidence and poise under pressure that I had never knowingly activated. That confidence, once understood, took me up into the alpine for the first time in my late fifties and to mountain summits, something I never imagined I would do. That confidence furnished me with the nerve to bring a group of friends together to assist me in my first attempt at a 100-mile weekend run—and believe that I would not leave everyone twiddling their thumbs if I petered out by mid-afternoon the first day. There was no room for self-doubt in those subsequent undertakings.

Despite all the hardships it presented, Bryce remains one of my most cherished race experiences. It's challenge to *leave it all out there* to get to safety—be that a finish line or an ambulance—held a mirror up to me like no other race.

CHAPTER 6

The Freezing & Chafing DNFs

After two summers of Covid race cancellations and deferrals, Canadian trail runners were all aflutter over the long-anticipated return of trail racing in the fall of 2021. Though the move to a mid-October weekend for the Squamish50 (the first departure from its historic August running) would mean darker starts and finishes, it would also give runners cooler days and less likelihood of breathing forest fire smoke. I welcomed the potential upsides of the change.

Then along came the atmospheric river with its headwaters in Hawaiian skies and its deluge point smack against the coastal mountainsides we were racing on.

"We'll get 180 millimetres, seven inches, or more at the airport from Thursday night through to the end of the event on Sunday afternoon," local meteorologist, and fellow run group member, Jason, communicated to the Capra gang. "More on the mountains."

I'd run in some pretty wet and cold conditions over the years, so for me the deluge presented a bit of a motivational challenge. As I organized my gear with the weather in mind, I also thought, *This is definitely going to be a weekend for new stories.*

———

October 16, 2021. Race Day.

Considering the weather conditions, I got everything right with my gear that morning. Absolutely everything. Except for the things I didn't.

Can you see what was about to go wrong?

———

3:15 a.m., wake up, shower, and poop attempt. 3:30 a.m., bowl of Cheerios: my trusted source of pre-race calories. Easy stretches. Easy thigh and calf roll. Final hydration pack check. Then I envision the race (a positive way of saying I fret over all the things I might not have done to prepare the crew plan and supplies). 4:00 a.m., attempt to poop again.

4:15 a.m., gear up for the Squamish50-Mile—race number one of the back-to-back 50/50.

Break out the Squirrel's Nut Butter to lube crotch and butt crack—do not be shy. "Fire in the hole!" only gets hotter when water is added on a long, wet race day. Pull on my favourite race-day Saxx sport underwear with the pouch. Maybe getting a bit worn around the edges, but they are acquainted with long days and tough conditions, having been in use for five years.

Under Armour compression short-sleeve base layer. No need to lube the nipples: shirts and pack never chafe with Under Armour against my skin.

Leggings. *Hmmm.* Two pairs, both black, lie before me: a thin skin-tight pair and a thicker loose-fitting warmer pair. The wind blows outside, whipping rain against the windows. We will climb past the 1,000-metre mark in today's race. Could be sleeting up there. Definitely going to be cold. I think of the skin-tight leggings in the wind and rain and shiver where I stand. The warmer set has been my friend on countless winter outings, running, hiking, snowshoeing. The pockets in them could come in useful for gloves and garbage too. I pull them on and make sure my upper base layer is lying flat beneath them.

On goes my long-sleeve running shirt. Another favourite. Its twin will be worn tomorrow in the 50K race. I zip up its high neck collar and pull a buff over it and fluff the buff around my neck. I love buffs. They are like comfort blankets on cold days, warming the neck, shielding the ears if needed, covering the nose and mouth in cold wind.

The yellow jacket I choose for the day is a cycling jacket with longer sleeves and a tail that drops low on my butt. It's a synthetic fleece-like material, and it's been with me for over fifteen years. How it hasn't fallen apart, I do not know. I zip up its high collar, and the buff beneath it hugs me. I feel prepared for the elements.

Mostly dressed, I force myself to partially undress and try for one final poop in the hope that putting my clothes on got things moving. Some success is encouraging; clean up and re-lube. Ultra-running is a messy, greasy affair, have no illusions otherwise.

It's 4:30 a.m. and I'm sitting on the bench in our front entry, applying Squirrel's Nut Butter to my heels, balls of my feet, and between, over, and around my toes. Over the grease, I pull on a once-washed pair of new Smartwool Merino crew socks with cushioned soles. Over those go my bright red Altra gaiters, pulled up to mid-calf, where they await my new slate-grey Altra Lone Peak trail runners (with more than 50 and less than 100 kilometres on them). Once the runners are on and tied, not too tightly, the gaiters drop to Velcro tabs and clip in place. I rarely go without gaiters on a long race or run; they keep the debris out and help me avoid the torturous hamstring and groin cramps that often come when removing shoes to get little rocks out deep in a race. With all the agonies available at the end of an ultramarathon, inflicting an avoidable shoe clean on taut and tired muscles and tendons is anathema to me. And today's rain is certain to provide plenty of mud splashes. The gaiters are a necessity.

My lightweight black Arc'teryx rain jacket with hood goes on next—a long-trusted piece of gear and an excellent final layer that protects against the cold wind as well. I wrestle my arms into my grey hydration pack, heavy with water and first fuels, spare lube, phone, whistle, space blanket, extra buff, and little bag of salt tabs.

I double-check that I have a little Ziploc stuffed in a pouch up near my left shoulder, pull it out, and hastily re-read my race-day runner plan. I mentally acknowledge its chronological bullet list of aid station time targets and the quantities of solid, chewy, gel, and liquid fuels I must consume between those aid stations. Red letters highlighting critical gear change and acquisition reminders jump out at me. Today, with this crap weather, my gear option list is longer than usual. I take comfort in knowing the crew plan mimics all this and more in much broader detail. They will help me.

Cindy comes to give me a hug and a kiss and to wish me luck. "Are you ready?" she asks.

"Hope so," I reply. It's not a good response. I want to know I'm ready, but the feeling is not there today. It concerns me.

I pull on a thin black 5 Peaks toque and then firmly set my white running cap over it. It's a snug fit and feels good. My green headlamp goes on as the crowning touch. Its elastic strap amps up my cap's snugness one last notch. I hop up and down and waggle my head side-to-side to see if the headlamp slips. It doesn't.

Black gloves with green pullover mitt-like covers round out my gear. I pull them on and Cindy opens the door. After I depart, she will get a few more hours of sleep, and then she's off to course marshal in the downpour. I say goodbye to thirteen-year-old golden retriever Kahlua. Half asleep, she's been lazily watching me from where she lies down the hall, not even hinting that I should take her out in that dejecting weather this early. *Smart girl.*

It's 4:45 a.m. Crew boss Suzanne is already waiting outside to take me to the start line.

Ready or not, here I go.

————

The rain dominates my senses in the starting corral. Gloved hands are already soaked and cold. Raindrops sparkle in headlamps and streetlights. Looking up, it's like we're in a snow globe of aquatic glitter. Beneath hundreds of wet feet, puddles glisten, and raindrops dance in flashes of reflected light. I listen to Race Director Gary Robbins' pre-race briefing, but I don't hear it. Instead, I hear the rain pelt off all the shifting and crinkling rain gear in a drumming of tiny thuds.

"Three. Two. One. GO!"

We're running. *Fifty miles to go.*

I've run 100 metres, and my breathing is already laboured. *Don't think about that.* Runners dodge puddles. Jump to the sides. Bump each other. *Stupid. Just run through them. Will you care about wet shoes ten hours from now? Will you jump then?*

"People, go through the damn puddles!" I want to shout. Then, like everyone else, I hop awkwardly over the next puddle and feel the strain on cold morning muscles and wish I'd listened to myself.

The Capra gang cheers me on at the first aid station. Solana and crew have owned this station for years, and happy volunteers in soaking-wet onesies and the craziness of the place give me a boost. The first 10 kilometres are done. Sachi greets me with his huge, patented grin as he directs runners toward the forest trail. It's his voice I recognize first, his face and body shape lost within the tent-like rain slicker he's shrouded in. Good to see him out as a course marshal.

Minutes later, I have two bad falls on the single-track heading to DeBeck's Hill. Slick roots leave me bruised both times. The mud on my leggings has a weight I didn't expect.

The pack thinned and stretched out early today. Twelve kilometres in, with many runners ahead, and quite a few behind, I'm already alone. *Why does pouring rain make the forest darker?* My world is no bigger than the moving orb of light projecting from my headlamp. The forest could end a few metres beyond my light bubble or go on for millions of miles.

Four years after my DeBeck's climb with Ann, the revenge runner, I'm back again under race conditions. Well, conditions of some sort. The normally dry Crouching Squirrel Trail is a stream—fast flowing and spraying over the rocks. Some sections are not recognizable in ankle-deep rushing water, and I trained on them. This is a DeBeck's climb like no other. Near the top, I'm finally able to turn my headlamp off and navigate by the gray, flat dawn light of the fall storm.

At Alice Lake aid station, Suzanne, in her bright green rain gear and blue toque, collects my fuel wrappers and hands me a baggie with my next round of calories. She checks my water reservoir. "You've had nothing to drink!" There's honest surprise in her voice.

"In this?" I hold my palms up to catch the rain.

"I know, but . . . you're 20 kilometres in."

"Just not thirsty. It's so wet!" I was thinking about how little I was drinking as I approached the aid station and checked my race-day running plan. Top up water, it said. *Nope, no need for that.* I berate myself for falling behind and promise Suzanne I will consume more water over the kilometres ahead. In conditions like this I know I will have to force the water down.

Suzanne takes a selfie of us, and I head out. I've got 32 kilometres to go before we meet again at Quest aid station.

Seventeen kilometres of mucky Garibaldi Highlands climbs and descents later, I'm at the Corners aid station and my drop bag for the second time before I head to the longest climb of the day. Pleased with my time and feeling as strong as I could hope for to this point—a very good sign given the fact that I've been fighting the mud, and it's been tiring—I make two decisions.

First, I add a second light green rain jacket under my Arc'teryx shell. I'm getting cold, and I have the Galactic Scheisse climb coming up. I've learned that a second rain jacket is a good insulator for keeping heat in. I don't care that it will keep sweat in as well—I've been soaked to the bone for hours already. I just need to make my wet clothes warmer, and the double-layer trick has worked for me in training.

Second, after much consideration during the loop that brought me back to this point, kilometres where my leggings got heavier and heavier, slipping down my butt at times with the weight of the water in them, I decide to keep them on for the ascent. I will change them at Quest where the thin pair I rejected earlier wait with the crew. I wrestle with the decision.

There's a reason I keep the baggy leggings on: a hypothermic DNF at the Diez Vistas 50K in 2019.

In that race, two-and-half years earlier, it hadn't taken many questions for the Tri-Cities Search and Rescue team at the 35-kilometre Eagle Mountain aid station to determine my DV50K was done. That cold afternoon I wasn't shivering anymore, and all I wanted to do was crawl under a tree and go to sleep. In fact, I had asked a runner—a baby-faced kid with a mop of tousled hair protruding this way and that from beneath his cap—to keep tabs on me and not let me do exactly that as we climbed to the aid station in the wind and rain. Sixteen kilometres earlier, at the Buntzen South aid station, I had chosen not to add an upper body layer, and Cindy and Jeanette, my mid-race crew that day, walked off the Diez Vistas course with my long-sleeved ticket to a finish while I ran off down the windblown trails getting colder and colder. I'd mistakenly believed the morning forecast that said I'd get hot that afternoon if I layered up. I should have listened to what my body was asking for in the moment—warmth.

Now, on the approach to Galactic Scheisse and determined to stave off the cold up high with waterlogged leggings, I chat with a runner who recently moved to the West Coast from Czechia. I assure him that the weather isn't always this bad. I also tell him about my first SQ50-Miler. "I had no dark moments," I tell him. "I was happy the whole day."

"I've never had a long race without dark moments," he replies. "And how are you doing today?"

"Good. I'm on pace in spite of this … rain." We jog down a hill toward a bridge with a creek raging below it, and my heavy leggings slide down my ass, uncomfortable and annoying. I don't tell him about my problem.

The Galactic climb starts. He powers away from me.

The leggings weigh a ton. Every lift of my knees feels like a workout, making Galactic twice as hard as it should be. They hang from my thighs like grandma's arm fat when I lift my knees to climb. I'm becoming agitated and consider taking them off and leaving them in a tree. *I can come up with friends next week and retrieve them*. But I don't act on this thought.

At the 40-kilometre halfway mark, there's a break in the trees with a view of the Squamish Valley down to Howe Sound. No view today with clouds less than a fatal leap away from the ledge. I find it odd to see three runners standing by the embankment across the trail from the cliff, shivering and stutter-stepping to stay warm. The skin on their legs is clammy white with red blotches. They tell me they're thinking of heading down and quitting if their friend doesn't catch up with them soon. Too cold.

I don't take the leggings off as the look of their skin reminds me too much of my Diez Vistas freezing DNF from thirty months ago.

My mind is in a dark place as I crest the trail's summit. I curse the cold, miserable in leggings that coat my knees and thighs like cement. There's a voice in my head screaming for this discomfort to all be over. To bolster my resolve, I scream back, *The entire weekend isn't even one-third done!* I jinxed myself an hour ago when I boasted I had no dark moments on my smiling SQ50-Mile back in 2017.

I start the long descent toward Quest on numb feet—frozen from the last seven hours spent in stream-like trails and multiple knee-deep creek crossings. My hands are also frozen, fingers stiff, already too useless to tear open a foil gel pack or re-tie a shoe. But my upper body is warm—my core is good. As motivation ebbs, I start to think about losing my 50/50 on day one. I assure myself that I made the right choice with the extra jacket. *I can drop the abominable pants down below at Quest, where it will be a few degrees warmer.* I note that the feeling is coming back to my feet as I slip and slide downhill. It's not much, but I'm grasping for anything to feel encouraged. One ounce of hope is all I need to outweigh the heavy burden of my water-logged clothing.

Halfway to Quest from the summit, I can't get my underwear to sit comfortably in my left crotch. I pull it down and out, but the discomfort isn't relieved.

I pass Cindy's course marshalling post and tell her everything is OK, even though it's not. She's upbeat and cheerful—fully immersed in her caregiving element on the course—encouraging everyone in this insufferable deluge, happy she got to 4x4 to this location up in the woods. I can tell she's enjoying herself, and I don't want to ruin her fun.

Ten minutes later, I'm through Word of Mouth, the aid station before Quest where Suzanne and crew await, 5 kilometres away. At this point, everything is wrong with my gear, from my waist to my ankles. The discomfort on the left of my scrotum has turned into pinpoint, horsefly-bite pain. I know exactly where my biggest problem is and I'm worried. On the steep downhills I pull my leggings and underwear away from my crotch with both hands to get some relief from whatever is scratching its way into me. I finally take off my left glove and put my hand into my pants to try to reorganize things. I withdraw it, fingers red with blood.

Dry underwear and leggings are less than 5 kilometres away. I press on. The pain can't be ignored. I stop and dig a dry buff out of my pack. I try to arrange it as a liner between my scrotum and underwear. There's no pain relief in that. I pull the bloody buff out and jam it in a pocket in my leggings. *What have I done?*

The consummate cheerleader for her Capra team, Solana meets me 300 metres outside of Quest. I know she'd been out in the downpour all day encouraging runners. I appreciate her so much. She is the running friend you want to finish for.

"I'm done," I tell her, and a terrible sadness overcomes me as I say it. It's like the spoken words make the feared thing come true. *Out of the 50/50 on day one. What a failure.* I'm fifty-nine years old. This is my hometown race and I want the finish so badly. I want to own a piece of this. *How will I ever regain the strength to get back here again?* I fight the tears.

"No. You're doing fine. Lots of time to cutoff. You've got nine hours done and you look great!" she laughs. "Crew is ready to go with hot noodles and dry clothes!"

"No, I'm really done." I can see by the look on her face that she knows I'm not joking. I can also see that she doesn't understand why. I'm on pace, and like always, I'm putting on a happy face for my friends. How could she know I'm afraid I'm about to lose a nut? And worse, how could she know that right here, right now, I'm terrified I'm losing my last chance to finish a 50/50?

Solana, in her blue rain slicker, gingerly leads me down the muddy trail to a ravine that's been dry as a bone every time I've crossed through it. Today the water is knee-deep and rushing loudly. Solana picks her way over rocks and fallen trees, trying not to submerge her feet. I consider her spidery route, realize how much pain will come from lifting my left leg like that, and slosh straight through the little river. *It can't make me any wetter.* I gave up trying to avoid the water and the muck long before daylight broke. Annie Johansen, longtime 5 Peaks volunteer coordinator, who completes the amazing Solana, Suzanne, Annie volunteer triumvirate, is on the far bank and takes a picture of me in the flood. It gets some traction online where I briefly become the poster boy for "drenched and done."

———

Suzanne will not accept my "I'm done." She shoves dry gear into my arms along with a towel. "Go change. Hurry up." She points to the restroom in the Quest campus building.

"You look strong," everyone keeps saying. "Dry off, lube up, new clothes will make you feel better. Your time is good. You've got this! We'll have your pack ready and noodles too." They know I love Jennie's noodles.

I cannot believe how heavy my gear is. Was it raining cement all morning? As each layer comes off, it falls with a resounding slap on the restroom floor. I sit on the toilet to examine the left side of my scrotum. I have a pea-sized hole oozing thick red/blue blood where I shouldn't have a hole.

I'm done.

The realization is numbing. How do I process this for myself?

The emotion that does well up is for my team. I'm suddenly overcome with grief for them. They're waiting outside, pumped up and ready to battle the elements until late tonight and excited to get up early tomorrow to do it all again just to get me across two finish lines. They believe I can do this—that's why they're here. They have their plans for dinners and coffees and huddling under umbrellas, and by getting me through these two days, they will win by successfully crewing two races that were hard and un-comfortable, yet deeply rewarding because they did it with—and for—their friends. And I'm about to take it away and shoot their fun all to hell. When I walk off the course, I take Suzanne, and her crew, and all the effort she put into this, with me. They have no choice—their race is finished when mine is.

I get up off the toilet seat, and, to my horror, it looks like a butcher's table. My heart races. *Where did all the blood come from?* The seat is smeared. The bowl is red. There's blood on the floor. I look at my legs for the first time and see that the insides and backs of my thighs have large sections with no skin. The back-sides are the worst, and my fingers slip on blood as I pull at my thighs to see how far around the damage goes. *How cold did I get? Why can't I feel this?*

What. Have. I. Done.

There's a knock on the restroom door.

"Sorry! Got a problem here. Be out in a bit!"

"OK," Annie calls back. "You've got lots of time to cutoff, but you really have to get moving." The crew's two-day plan is still alive and well, and they are energized to get me going.

What a disaster. My chafing DNF.

———

The primary lesson learned that day: Nacho Libre was wrong.

Cinematically astute readers will recall that Nacho famously said, "When you are a man, sometimes you wear stretchy pants in your room. It's for fun." On October 16, 2021, I discovered that wearing stretchy pants wasn't just for fun, it was a necessity—especially when I was out in an atmospheric river. My big mistake when gearing up that morning was to leave the thin, stretchy pants behind. Subsequent disaster reconstruction done on my red, raw nether regions clearly showed where the pocket seams of my baggy running pants had turned into moving saw blades, in places acting in concert with my older, ragged-edged underwear to auger away numb skin and drill holes. Thin, tight stretchy pants coupled with newer skintight athletic underwear would have prevented my problem. That simple combination solved my wet weather chafing problems thereafter.

But what about my concern for the cold? Would I have risked another hypothermic DNF at the top of Galactic if I'd donned stretchy pants pre-race, or doffed my soggy leggings mid-race? No. My concerns over the pants were misplaced. What I learned instead was that in cold race conditions where I was continually moving, keeping my core warm was the key, followed by head, hands and arms, and lastly, legs. If I took care of the trunk, the branches would take care of themselves. Covering up my legs would do little to improve my temperature regulation performance in a race. Had I understood that descending order of coverage on the weekend of the deluge, I might have captured that 50/50.

When I put this lesson together with the cooling tricks I learned from my flaming DNF, I saw complete alignment. In both extremes, hot and cold, if I addressed core temperature first, then head, then arms/hands, my legs could receive minimal attention. At the 50/50, I took care of my core—very well—but I incorrectly, and destructively addressed my legs.

Over the years, I would sometimes think back to the afternoon I spotted that first trail runner who blew past me in the winter woods above our old neighbourhood. I would compare what he and I were wearing, both out for a day on a chilly hill. I always knew I had a strong tendency to overdress—it was a product of my Saskatchewan prairie upbringing where temperatures dropped well beneath forty-below. One night I had to walk to a farmhouse after an incident with a post-midnight car in a ditch to avoid freezing to death. As I progressed in my ultrarunning life, I struggled against my prairie history in an effort to become the lightly dressed loony. I got myself in trouble at the rainswept 50/50 because on day one I remained a bit too much me, and not enough him. Whereas at the chilly DV50K I was too much him. And farther back at burning Bryce I was too much me again. It was complicated. Who did I need to be to survive all the changing conditions in the wild?

Ultimately, figuring out who I needed to be as an ultra-runner was not the solution to my "gear problems." I didn't have an identity crisis. I was making bad layering decisions guided by erroneous assumptions about how to dress an active hot or cold or soaking athletic body. I might have survived the 50/50 had I layered down my legs—because I had my core nicely taken care of, and losing the pants when my gut told me to pitch them up into a tree would have eliminated the chafing. I might have survived the DV50 had I layered up my core—because my core was freezing. I knew that when I saw Cindy and Jeanette, but I let my concerns about the future override what I needed in the present. I might have survived the Bryce Canyon 50K had I layered down my core—because my core was boiling. But there was a lot going wrong that day, and I didn't yet have the core cooling skills that would have gotten me the rest of the way. Bryce might not have been salvaged with one little gear change. So many lessons learned.

———

Forethought and crew/race plans with gear layering options and red flags have gone a long way in helping me overcome the layering mistakes that made for some epic DNFs. Ultra-races allow drop-bags and crews for a reason. I've learned to use both for layering.

I've also learned that sometimes I don't have to change who I am to fix something. Maybe I just have to change the one thing I consistently do wrong to make outcomes better across the board.

Other lessons learned: lube more and go seamless.

While I don't think any amount of lube would have saved my crotch from the tandem action of old nubby underwear being ground into my skin by heavy, wet, and moving pocket seams, lube on the friction points at the base of my Saxx boxers might have staved off the worst of the deep abrasions that resulted on my thighs.

My chafing DNF taught me to think differently about my gear and to consider points of contact where clothes and packs moved in different directions over skin. In those places, I began lubing more generously. If conditions worsened, especially with heat and wetness, additional focus on preventing friction became critical for keeping me in the game.

Lighter, seamless underwear and leggings (seamless everything!) were essential for the HomeRun100 that followed my 50/50 chafe-out. In fact, with re-lubing I made it through all thirty-plus sweaty hours in one pair of underwear, no chafe. I became a picky ginch shopper in my old age after learning the benefits of wearing skintight athletic garments—under baggier shorts and shirts, of course. I didn't get the moniker "Captain Muffin Top" for no reason.

Finally, for comfort's sake alone, I made two gear adjustments after my October 2021 DNF: new Crest ADV Hybrid Weather Gloves with waterproof mitt covers and a Pukka waterproof running cap. These made a world of difference to my level of comfort long hours into wet, cold runs.

Following the October 50/50, training for my 100-miler took place over one of the coldest winters Squamish had seen in years. The waterproof mitts, much like my waterproof shell, not only protected my hands against wetness but also against the cold wind. Waterproof gear served me well as an insulator, too, although I'm not sure that those who run hot would agree. I run cold, so I've always enjoyed being a bit toasty inside my gear. Many runners I've spent time with on the trail run hot, and at the end of a run, it's been comical to see me in jacket, toque, and gloves beside them and their steaming bare arms.

Ultimately, all runners must decide for themselves what gear works for them on regular days and on highly abnormal days. The purpose of sharing these DNF stories—flaming, freezing, chafing— is to illustrate that I made disastrous gear layering choices, and from those failures, I learned lessons that improved my performance in subsequent events.

And, like Nacho, I needed to let the world know that sometimes when you are a man, you wear stretchy pants. It's for fun . . . and more.

Things the Trail Taught Me

Inevitably, new trail runners hanging with the sweeper at the back of the Saturday morning Capra Trail Running Club ask, "How did you do it?"

CHAPTER 7

Know Thy Fuelling Self

By the time we reached the small, barren settlement of Lobuche, on our Everest Base Camp trek in 2015, my body decided it needed saving. At an elevation of 16,210 feet, and in distress, it chose to turn off non-essential organs, like my gut, and dedicate energy derived from the consumption of my muscles to power me back down the Khumbu Valley to a place where I could safely inhale more oxygen. The problem was that my conscious mind had every intention of pressing on to the top of Kala Patthar, at 18,519 feet, one more day away. That would be our Himalayan summit and give us our best view of Everest to the east, across the Khumbu glacier where Everest Base Camp lay at the foot of the icefall far below us. At 16,000 feet, my mind was set on adventure; my body, set on escape.

Squeezed into the tightly packed, plywood-panelled dining hall of our ramshackle Lobuche lodge, with an appetite registering less than zero, and watching all the acclimatized trekkers and climbers around me wolfing down their dal bhat, meat stews, and golden-brown macaroni, I was introduced to a body I didn't know—and that body happened to be my own.

Few of us know our physical selves above 16,000 feet. And in the context of ultrarunning, I'd say few people are aware of who they are after 30 kilometres on their feet, or 50 kilometres, or 100 kilometres, or 100 miles, and more so, few people are aware that they can be physically different people at each of those distances. We are shapeshifters, and in this case, shapeshifting describes how the functioning of our physiology changes relative to elevation and distance increases.

If we say that people go to the mountains or run ultras to find themselves, I guess this is one way to literally flesh out that concept. I have discovered a variety of physically different Randys at higher elevations and longer distances. But I digress. My intention with this story was to share important news about Nepalese macaroni, and I should get back to that.

For trekkers already acclimatized to extreme altitudes, like those I watched happily chowing down at our Lobuche lodge, Nepalese macaroni made a nutritious meal. But for me, whose body had decided it was dying, it became a notorious bomb.

I came to understand the dichotomous nature of Nepalese macaroni the following day when we reached the even more barren Gorak Shep, elevation 16,942 feet, around noon. Hunkered down in another dimly lit lodge, trying to warm up from the morning's trek that passed beneath the west face of Nuptse, possibly the most glorious mountain I had ever viewed, I spotted a plate of steaming macaroni a few tables away. My gut did not turn as I stared at it, even with the pungent spices sharp in my nose—a promising sign. I asked Pemba, our much-loved guide, if I should order some. With a "trust me" look on his face (having witnessed hundreds of other trekkers whose bellies seethed in soured turmoil), he pulled a crumpled box of fragmented baby's digestive cookies from his pack and set them on the table in front of me. I, having matured beyond baby cookies, and overcome with the thought of warm noodles refortifying my dwindling strength, ordered the macaroni. Pemba's warm smile wished me well.

There was no single trail up near the summit of Kala Patthar, it was a wind-swept jumble of rock and ice where the path of least resistance changed from day to day. Therefore, when I tucked myself behind a boulder, hidden from Pemba, and exploded out my backside, I had set myself up to be crouched, with pants around ankles and face all a grimace, pretty much at centre stage for a group of American trekkers who popped up over the stone pile directly in front of me, and who passed, one-by-one, delivering more than a few sympathetic pats to my shoulder. My guess was that none of them felt inclined to order the macaroni that night, considering the show I put on for them in that frigid stone theatre.

Though not funny at the time, the story of my intestinal theatrics later elicited the loudest laughter from Kushan and Tende, our young Sherpa porters. I recall that when I shared how my poor fuelling choice had derailed the American trekking train's enjoyment of Chomolungma, the Mother Goddess, who rose majestically across the valley from my agony, one of the boys ended up on all fours pounding the floor of our Pheriche lodge with one hand. Apparently, potty humour crossed cultural boundaries and partial language barriers with ease.

My stomach turned off for four days at high altitude, and I lost thirteen pounds, most of it upper body muscle. Cindy and Jeanette also dealt with headaches along with their loss of appetite, both maladies being common for ascending trekkers in that region. None of us suffered from high-altitude cerebral edema (HACE) or high-altitude pulmonary edema (HAPE), although we did encounter two emergency evacuations triggered by those conditions: one a trekker and the other a porter. Seeing a Nepalese porter affected so traumatically by HACE at high elevation served as a reminder that what may not affect a person under extreme conditions on one day can bring them crashing down without warning in the future. No one could claim immunity from the ailments of extreme adventuring just because they had been at high altitudes or gone long distances before. The dangers returned afresh each new morning.

I experienced my own sliding scale of unanticipated physical breaking points as I pushed the distances on my journey to go far in my fifties, closer to sea level. And at each breaking point, I discovered a physical me I hadn't previously known. Finding out who, or what, I became at those progressive distances became the key to going farther.

———

While training for my first 50K in the spring/summer of 2015, I had a 30-kilometre route that I could do with a few snacks, or on a cool day totally unfuelled, and a 35-kilometre route where I repeatedly depleted all my energy reserves on the same descending trail at the 32-kilometre mark, barely able to make it home regardless of how many granola bars I desperately consumed. And once I was in the calorie deficit hole, there was no way I was going to crash-fuel my way out of it by starting the fuelling process at the point of the fall. That, apparently, was the top limit of my poorly fuelled physical self, which is exactly what I discovered during my first marathon when I abruptly bonked and crashed in Stanley Park.

Wanting to complete an ultramarathon, I needed to remove my 32-kilometre bonk roadblock, so I dug into the literature and quickly discovered the solution: I must start fuelling after the first hour and continue at a constant rate of 200-250 calories per hour without fail.

For me to be successful past 32 kilometres, continual adequate fuelling that started after the first hour was the only method that would keep me out of the inescapable hole, hours later. This simple rule sustained me all the way to 100 miles, apart from when I broke it in the midnight hours of my HomeRun100 and dug a pit for myself that only crew heroics could extract me from.

But learning how many calories per hour I needed was only the beginning because my body shapeshifted as the distances increased. After 40 kilometres, I became a whole new animal who retched out what the under-40-kilometre me could stomach. As a result, I didn't just need to know *how many* calories per hour to consume, I also needed to know *what form* of calories would stay in as my distances increased.

It was a bit of a shocker to experience this on my first two 50K races when all the solid foods I had trained with to distances up to 35 kilometres physically shot out of me for the final 10 kilometres of both races. I finished much more fatigued than if I had been able to keep calories going in until the end. I eventually learned about all those gels other runners ate in the process of figuring out how to get past my end-of-ultra energy bar up-chuck.

After years of trial and error, I learned to manage 50K races and training runs by fuelling with solids early, switching to chewy/gummy calories in the middle, consuming gels toward the end, and sipping water all the way. But then, around 60 kilometres, I shape-shifted again, and even the gels ceased to work as my primary calorie source.

At times I wondered if my step-by-step tummy shutdown on a long run was connected to how my body went into escape mode and shut down my gut on our Himalayan adventure. In a race that kept me moving for more than ten hours, and sometimes upwards of thirty hours, I could only assume that my body flipped into survival mode, shut my gut down, and dedicated all energy expenditures to getting to safety; that assumption being based on literature that indicated that digestion suppression was one of the first mechanisms activated in fight or flight, and stress. The deeper I got into an ultramarathon, the more likely one or all three factors would trigger a digestive shutdown.

Thankfully, after a difficult period of putting fuel in and having it fly out, I found a solution to my post-60-kilometre escape-mode tummy issues: a steady flow of liquid calories starting way back at the 40-kilometre mark. Not only did the liquid calories give me the ongoing energy I needed, but they seemed to make other fuel, like chewy calories and gels, and aid station food, more palatable as time went on. Bonus! Perhaps those liquid calories forced my digestive system to stay turned on with sips taken every five-to-ten minutes? While my lay-runner gut feel fully acknowledged that I might be dealing with a placebo effect, the introduction of liquid calories early in a long ultra helped me eat other foods beyond the 50-mile mark. It worked, so I stuck with it.

When I look back at my HomeRun100 middle-of-the-night crash, I see all these factors in play. The inevitable nausea of going more than 100 kilometres began; I cut back on my liquid calorie intake to avoid the nausea because I was having fun; this caused my tummy to start shutting down; with an upset stomach I started to fake eating my chewies and gels; greater nausea developed because I was depleted; I cascaded to a crash. Then, with the help of the crew, I religiously sipped my liquid calories, turned my tummy back on and slowly rebuilt my calories to the point where most of my crash symptoms retreated. Donut bites and pickles once again became palatable, and I returned to moving with purpose.

Over the years, I experimented with a variety of fuelling drinks and mixes, but it wasn't until I read Cory Reese's *Nowhere Near First: Ultramarathon Adventures From The Back Of The Pack* and *Into the Furnace* that I turned to Tailwind Endurance Fuel. Reese consumed some crazy foods like bean burritos, ice cream, Twinkies, and Ding Dongs during his 100-mile races, and he ran a lot of them, but the one constant I saw was Tailwind. And while the only thing I had in common with Cory Reese was that I, too, was nowhere near first in any of my ultramarathons, I must say that sipping Tailwind early and regularly did for me what it appeared to do for him: kept his stomach activated enough to eat whatever he wanted to at aid stations and the drive-thrus he walked up to.

Reading from the package: "Tailwind. All you need. Really. Endurance fuel. Complete energy, electrolytes, hydration. Mix 2-3 scoops with 590-710ml water per hour for longer efforts. Light, clean taste. Easy on your gut. Mixes clear, rinses clean. No fake stuff."

It became the game-changer for me.

With Tailwind I had a way to keep my hydration going, sip by sip, while at the same time keeping my gut functioning with a constant flow of calories. At the Javelina Jundred 100K (four years after my big Lobouche shutdown), the first long race where I used Tailwind as my base calories throughout the race, I had zero fuelling issues. Even better, I became an aid station calorie consumer like never before.

Granted, part of my ability to consume calories at that race might have had something to do with how well Aravaipa, the company who staged the events, stocked their aid stations, but never had I been able to eat PB&J, and quesadillas, and pumpkin pie, at any point in a race after 25 kilometres, let alone the 94-kilometre mark. On my last pass through Rattlesnake Aid Station, I literally pigged out (javelina'd?) before moving with purpose to the finish line, sipping my Tailwind under the velvet black canopy of a desert night sky dotted with pinpoint stars. Happy tummy; happy runner.

———

I just explained how I figured out how to fuel my body, not your body. But the one thing I guarantee is that if you want to go far— ultramarathon far—you will need to discover who you become with regard to fuel and hydration the farther you go. Furthermore, I would put money on it that you need to find your new shape-shifting self multiple times before you figure out what will go in, and stay in, beyond the distances of your typical training runs.

And remember, when you're way up in the mountains, pushing yourself far past your physical boundaries, and someone in the know tells you to eat the baby's digestive cookies and not the macaroni, listen to them.

CHAPTER 8

Four-and-One for Success

Jacquelyn Janzen was an important pacer on my HomeRun100: she put in 62 kilometres that weekend. Consistent, funny, stern, and strong, she would also acknowledge that she suffers from an ongoing disbelief that she can do what she does—regardless of what she's done in the past. I, too, suffer from an ongoing lack of faith in myself, and I know other ultrarunners who congregate in the little church of blessed self-doubters. Despite past victories and thousands of training kilometres, we approach each race event with an abject fear of failure. Hallelujah.

The day prior to my 100-miler, Jacquelyn and I were talking about our shared inability to unwaveringly believe in ourselves when I handed her the April 2022 edition of *UltraRunning Magazine.* "Check out the Gary Cantrell article, 'Fear of Failure,'" I said. "He put my head in the right place for this weekend."

Cantrell: "'Start slow or you will collapse later.' Doesn't sound particularly threatening. But consider the message it carries. It translates to, 'Don't try too hard, or you will fail.' Now, let's take the same basic idea in a different form, `Pace yourself conservatively early, so you can finish strong.'

"The same truth underlies both versions," Cantrell writes. "Knowing how to pace yourself is the key to doing well. But the first version is an admonishment to be careful or you will fail, and the second is the advice to run a smart race so you can succeed. Sometimes a message can be subtle. But it does not have to be overt to put your mind in the wrong place. There is a truth here that is known in every sport: you cannot win by playing not to lose."

Jacquelyn and I discussed Cantrell's doctrine in light of our proclivity to put our minds in a place of fear at the start of our races, doubting the outcome rather than looking ahead to a strong finish, with the goal of strategizing our way toward that positive outcome.

Jacquelyn read Cantrell's conclusion out loud, and we both agreed to embrace it the next day. "Set yourself free and let go of that fear. Next time you toe the line, don't start slow to avoid collapse. Pace wisely from the start, so that you can finish strong. Don't run away from failure; run toward success."

The following morning when Jacquelyn paced me through kilometres 10 to 35 of my HomeRun100, we focused on maintaining a pacing strategy she had taught me years before. I like to think we ran and hiked *toward success* the whole way.

———

My best friend Glenn is my twin brother from a different mother—we share the same birth date, July 1, 1962. My goal was to go 100 continuous miles on my own two feet by the time we reached our sixtieth birthdays in 2022. His goal, every day, is to walk just far enough to get life's tasks done. Glenn has multiple sclerosis, and he's my role model for perseverance. He is also Jacquelyn's dad.

In 2013, Jacquelyn hatched a plan to raise money for MS in support of her dad, and lupus in support of her friend, Savannah. We all thought she'd cracked when she told us her idea: never having run a marathon in her life, she said she was going to run twelve marathons in the span of seventeen days the following summer—over 500 kilometres and the entire length of Vancouver Island from Port Hardy to Victoria. Yup, that was the plan. *Embrace the Race* was the name she gave her event. None of us knew how she would get it done.

Jacquelyn trained. She trained more. She trained smarter. She and her family planned. The woman ran a dozen marathons in seventeen days. People were inspired and donated. And many wondered, *How did she do it?*

I ran with Jacquelyn on one of those marathons, and I saw how she did it.

Four-and-one.

Jacquelyn used a pacing formula that enabled her to finish strong, over and over again, marathon after marathon, day after day.

Four minutes running, one minute hiking. Over and over.

The day I ran with her, she executed that formula religiously, and I converted.

Four-and-one became my pacing strategy for the early runnable sections of every ultramarathon I ran thereafter. I learned to trust it because I had tested the alternative—running continually early on in every runnable section—in training runs up to 50 kilometres. At my age and level of fitness, I discovered that I could not go much beyond 50 kilometres if I ran continually from the start. But I could go up to 100 miles if I started with *four-and-one* in the runnable sections early in the game, and then shifted to *three-and-two* when I felt the need to conserve a bit more energy as the race progressed. Evidence of the improvements I derived from that strategy was seen when I analyzed my pace deep into my long training days when *three-and-two* rendered my overall pace quicker, for longer.

The big payoff came when I implemented that pacing strategy in my HomeRun100 and posted my fastest 50-mile and 100K times *ever.* In its simplest form, *four-and-one* became, for me, a numeric representation of what the tortoise did when it raced the hare.

Jacquelyn got me running toward success with *four-and-one* eight years before we read the Cantrell article. Our problem was that we were pacing ourselves to avoid failure rather than doing it to achieve success. We changed that perception in our heads in April 2022.

———

"Practicing for the end of your race? Why?" a trail runner asked when he matched my pace to chat for a few hundred metres of my speed hike.

"Because I'm slow and I'm going to be out there a long time."

"Huh."

Practicing to consistently hike at pace for long periods of time is a foreign concept to many runners—unless you're a forever back-of-the-packer like me, in which case, it's essential. *Four-and-one* became my most effective strategy for pacing wisely at the start of an ultramarathon—thank you, Jacquelyn. The most useful strategy for managing a hiking pace at the end of my races became: *move with purpose*—thank you, Jennie.

In the same way that I stacked my 100-mile pacing team by putting Jacquelyn up front where I trusted her to deliver on *four-and-one* early in the game, I placed Jennie at key sections of my journey because she was a well-seasoned pacer who could tell me, "You're moving with purpose, keep it up," with remarkable effect.

Moving with purpose. As an ultramarathoner, deep in an event, when running had already ceased many kilometres ago and my legs felt like long rusty hinges and walking was all I had available to me in the final kilometres, being congratulated for *moving with purpose* was one of my best motivators.

When I entered the sport, I was intrigued by the fact that ultra-runners were able to hike to the end and still pull off an official finish. Then I discovered how much effort it took to hike at a reasonable pace for a long time. Coincidentally, I also learned that hiking alone wasn't the answer, keeping the creaking hinges from seizing up was the key, and the oil that kept my hinges from ceasing to swing turned out to be a purposeful mind.

I first heard Jennie use that line on Jen's "50 Miles on My Favourite Trails" in 2021. I instantly embraced it as a mantra because *moving with purpose* encapsulated strategy as much as mindset. Strategically it expressed physical pace while at the same time expressing mental determination. The mantra encompassed physical and mental consistency. It was how I came to define where I wanted my mind and body to be when I enter the *ultrarunner's pain cave* late in a race. When I was moving through hell, I had to keep on . . . moving with purpose.

If you are a half-marathon runner, or marathoner, or maybe a 50K runner who can finish that ultra quickly in under six hours, I challenge you to consistently hike at 6 kilometres per hour for five straight hours. Try to hike 30 kilometres, no running, at a pace that is consistent each and every hour, and then tell me you're not feeling different muscle pain than what you experience if you run that distance.

The first time you do it, I bet you're wrecked the next day and discover all kinds of vengeful little muscles you never knew you had. That's because we use different muscles when we speed hike than when we run. For a back-of-the-packer like me, this is what I'm faced with at the end of all my ultramarathons: hours of speed hiking. So I train for them. On my training plans, many of my 30-kilometre Sundays are all about speed hiking—practicing for the end of the race. That training teaches my body to move at a pace that can be maintained by muscle memory, for hours. At the end of an ultra, as long as muscle memory remains, I can continue moving with purpose because I've trained myself to do it, and I know what the mental determination needed to sustain that motion feels like.

Hiking fast gave me my first 50K, and hiking fast gave me my first 100K. In both races, I lost my ability to run because IT band issues crippled my knees. I couldn't run, but I could hike with purpose, and I did, all the way to those finish lines.

————

On my Bryce Canyon 50K, before I started heatstroke barfing, I met a 100-mile runner on the trail who was chugging along at a brisk walking pace.

"I don't run," he said. "I speed hike. Can't run at all. My knees are wrecked."

"And you make cutoff?" I queried, a bit perplexed that he was hiking *the whole way*.

"Oh yeah. Three miles per hour is all you need, man. Three miles per hour finishes an ultra."

The math is simple. One hundred miles divided by a thirty-hour cutoff is 3.33 miles per hour. So he's right if you leave out what's behind the decimal point, and that missing amount can be regained on the downhills.

Three miles per hour for an American gets it done. Five kilometres per hour for a Canadian gets it done too. Five is bigger so, obviously, Canadians go faster.

Back-of-the-packers, if you *four-and-one* to pace wisely at the beginning, and if you train to move purposefully for several hours at 5 to 6 kilometres per hour toward the end, you're going to earn your ultramarathon finisher medal on many racecourses. As for nastier courses with lots of elevation, well, that's where focused climb training comes in.

————

Being able to run/hike faster does not make you a better climber. Being able to climb stronger makes you a faster runner/hiker. That's been my experience. The hills are my friends.

When I switched gears in the spring of 2022 and started training specifically for the very hilly Squamish50/50, after a full block of training for my less hilly 100-miler, I was surprised to discover that during my non-climbing rest weeks I would set personal bests (PBs) on my flatter 10-kilometre routes without trying. The weeks of grind-it-out climbing had made me faster when I went for an easy run. Although I understood the principle behind it, I had never seen results as obvious as the PBs I bashed out in that training block.

Building climbing strength was a critical strategy for my success. As a runner who chases cutoffs, how many people have I passed on the final climbs of my races who lacked the strength to keep climbing consistently? A lot. Where have I faltered most? On the final climbs. Where have I excelled the most? On the final climbs, when I've trained well for them. It's eerie how close to 5 kilometres per hour I fast hike when I'm moving with rhythmic, arm-swinging-purpose across rolling terrain and then pressing my palms down on my quads on the steep climbs.

There's a flipside of climb training that's important: once I get up to the top, I get to train for the downhills at the end of my races, too. This seems obvious—what goes up must come down—but it's *how* I come down that is important: I practice coming down with purpose. On my long-run training days, I always try to put a climb at the end with a reasonably steep downhill that forces me to practice ultra-shuffling downward on sore, tired legs. It is a gross thing to do, but it pays off. Muscle memory is critical at the end of races, and downhill muscle memory requires repetition in training because it needs to happen when my legs are in pain. Even a tender descent is going to hurt. So I move down each final training descent as if a cutoff is nipping at my heels.

Also, I vary descent training between technical trails and long forest roads. Why? Because technical descents help me figure out how to remain agile when I'm in pain, and forest roads repetitiously beat me up if I add some speed and really pound them. If I do both from time to time, with adequate recovery in between, I am able to survive both types of descents on race day and move again with purpose on the next uphill that follows.

My friend Amish Solanki was training for his first 50K while I was training for my 50/50. We teamed up to work the hills, and as we pounded down steep forest service roads together, we would comment on how much the punishment sucked. In September 2022, Solana and I, and some other friends from the Capra Trail Running Club, crewed Amish's race. I still recall the panic we went through when we realized how fast he was moving on the hills—uphill and downhill! It was all we could do to race to our upcoming crew location to keep up with him.

His training to climb and descend with purpose had made Amish stronger and faster. Big time! He kicked his first ultramarathon, the very difficult WAM 50K run up and over two mountains in Whistler, BC, with strong climbing legs. As a first ultra, that was impressive.

CHAPTER 9

Don't Quit—and Why that's BS

I don't get hung up on other people's opinions. Much.

That said, I must share a hang-up I have with what other people say from time to time about ultrarunning. I don't do well with non-runners whose eyes brighten at any mention of an ultramarathon and say, "I know how to finish those. Don't quit!"

———

I confess I fell prey to the uninformed *don't quit* mindset early in my ultrarunning life. As I considered going far on my feet, it appeared to me that sheer determination and a no-holds-barred approach to physical suffering were the strategies to get it done. *No matter what, don't quit. That will earn me an ultra finish.*

Then I read the best prescriptive running book currently on my bookshelf: Sarah Lavender Smith's *The Trail Runner's Companion*. This is a book every runner who aspires to go far should own, read, and return to repeatedly. In my mind, Lavender Smith totally debunked the stand-alone notion of *don't quit*. Instead, what I derived from her input was a *know when to quit* approach that I've used to my advantage, both physically and mentally.

Using Lavender Smith's four reasons *to quit* I put together a logical *if-then* list of my own *personal quit criteria* ranked in order of importance. When considered in terms of potential real-life outcomes, the list frames the extreme sport of ultrarunning in an ominous way.

If I am risking life and limb with a problem like heat stroke or altitude sickness, *then* I will quit.

If I am asymmetrically walking and it gets worse if I try to run, *then* I will quit.

If I am unable to digest calories or take in fluids due to upset stomach and still have more than four hours to go in my race, *then* I will quit.

If this is a B-race leading up to my season's A-race and if I'm at risk of exacerbating an injury that will keep me from my A-race, *then* I will quit.

If none of my quit criteria are met, *then* Randy, *DON'T QUIT*!!!

There is enough raw power in a course of logic like this, when compared to the simple statement "Don't quit," that it's worth unpacking.

Standing alone with no context, *don't quit* is nebulous at best, dangerous at worst. It is so dangerous that it's BS, in my opinion. The clearest examples of why *don't quit* choices must be made within a framework of *when to quit* conditions lie in the mountaineering books that line my library shelf. Those books hold story after story of accomplished climbers who, after days and weeks of pushing for a summit, turned back a hundred metres or less from the mountain top because they met a quit condition that could not be bypassed. That same shelf also contains the stories of many climbers who didn't quit when an "*If* I go farther than this *then* I will die" condition was met, and who perished.

Let's start with the criterion of greatest importance. If I am risking life and limb in an ultra-race, I will quit. I have real-life examples of heatstroke, hypothermia, and vicious chafing that each developed into quit conditions. Two of those problems put me in danger of risking my life, the other, a "limb" I prefer not to talk about. I am forever grateful that I quit at the Bryce Canyon Ultra and did not carry on up Thunder Mountain Trail. I would have seriously injured myself trying to go those last 13 kilometres. *Don't quit* made no sense in that ultramarathon context.

If I am asymmetrically hiking/walking and the condition worsens when I run, then quit. This one is impactful for me. If I am limping when I walk, I will quit the race because injury will result. But if I can move with purpose at 5 kilometres per hour with a symmetrical gate, DON'T QUIT!

Do you see the power of having a precise pre-existing measuring stick to help make mid-race decisions? As mentioned in the last chapter, I hiked to the finish of my first 50K and first 100K because IT band issues caused me to run asymmetrically in a ton of pain but allowed me to hike symmetrically. How cool is that? I got my Javelina Jundred buckle because Sarah Lavender Smith established parameters I could use to gauge when I should not quit. Thank you, Sarah.

If *when to quit* was a nebulous "I'll see in the moment" thing in my mind that day, I might have quit Javelina when I couldn't run anymore. Wouldn't that have been sad?

If I am unable to digest calories or take in fluids due to upset stomach and still have more than four hours to go in my race, I quit. To not quit, and to force my body to the end of something like that, could have long-term consequences for my health like kidney failure from excessive dehydration.

Ultras are not to be trifled with. But the flip side is equally important. Day one of my 2022 Squamish50/50 (a story yet to be told) was a hot one, and it beat me up terribly. When I got to the last aid station with 10 kilometres to go, my stomach was no longer taking in calories or fluids, and I knew it wasn't going to reset that night. But I only had two hours to go at 5 kilometres per hour, and I knew I was trained well enough, and my mind was focused enough, to hold that pace to the end. So, I didn't quit and got the finish that night even though I lost six pounds over the course of the race.

My fourth quit criterion pits long-term vision against short-term satisfaction. If I'm in a B-race leading up to my season's A-race and if conditions in the B-race put me at risk of exacerbating an injury that keeps me from my A-race, then I will quit. Been there, done that. When the 60K Sweat leg of the Golden Ultra Blood, Sweat, and Tears stage race was causing havoc with my post-appendix-surgery tummy, my Javelina Jundred was four weeks away. Golden was my B-race. Javelina my A-race. I called it quits 40 kilometres into Sweat and captured my first 100K a month later as a result. Again, can you imagine if I had pushed Golden with a *don't quit* mentality? I surely would have lost both finishes. I'm ever so happy I pulled out of the first race to rattle down Mount 7 in an old pickup and get plopped at the finish line to drink beer with Jen's partner, Derek, and watch everyone else bring home their victories. Nothing lost for me. Everything gained. I traded a DNF in September for my first 100K buckle in October.

To date, Lavender Smith's four conditions have worked for me as the criteria for my decisions to walk off of ultramarathon racecourses and, more importantly, to stay on them, even though I was overwhelmed by fatigue, discomfort, boredom, and pain. When you are sitting in the comfort of your home you need to make the calm, calculated determinations of what your personal quit criteria will be in your next ultra. You shouldn't be guessing at what constitutes those conditions out on the racecourse. And then, when none of your quit criteria are met, no matter how lousy or tired you feel, *DON'T QUIT*.

And while you're sitting there doing that, perhaps grab a second piece of paper and jot down a few personal quit criteria for some of those work, business, and relational ultras you're currently running. It's quite possible that some *if, then, quit* and *DON'T QUIT* logic can help you with difficult decisions that feel nebulous because they lack the right framework. I know I've migrated this thinking elsewhere to good effect—particularly my business life. Just a thought.

———

I would like to expand on why I think a *don't quit* mentality is dangerous.

My choice to not pull out of the Bryce Canyon 50K at Thunder Mountain Aid haunts me: I could have quit the race at a water source, with capable people nearby, and an eventual car ride out when I first considered stopping, but I didn't. After that, if it wasn't for the ants that put me over the top in terms of discomfort and aggravation, I wonder if I would have made the choice to self-rescue when I did, or if I would have held onto the *don't quit* mentality that pushed me, already suffering heatstroke, kilometres past a safe escape and toward an unattainable finish line. Would I have ended up being treated on the course by those military medics? Worse? There was talk at our hotel of runners in the hospital after that meltdown.

There's a touchstone book in my library called *Deep Survival* by Laurence Gonzales—it's about who lives, who dies, and why, in extreme conditions. One of the concepts that grabbed me when I first read the book was the human habit of making mental maps. We map our environments, we map our careers, we map our relationships. In many areas of our lives, we instinctively map/plan to see our futures, just like I consciously map out my training and race-day running plans to get to the finish line.

According to Gonzales, disaster happens when something traumatic occurs that throws a roadblock into our mapped-out mental plan and we proceed with the plan anyway and become lost.

Often, this defines who dies in the mountains, in business, and metaphorically speaking, in relationships. "The human brain is particularly well suited to making complex plans that have an emotional component to drive motivation and behaviour. Plans are stored in memory just as past events are. *To the brain, the future is as real as the past.* The difficulty begins when reality doesn't match the plan" (*Deep Survival*, italics are mine).

At Bryce Canyon, my plan to get to the finish line had an emotional component that drove motivation, and that's a good thing. It enabled me to envision the race and push through my training to get there ready to go. The problem was that my brain also saw all that training as an investment that wasn't to be squandered with a quit, and that's what pushed me out of Thunder Mountain Aid and toward a future finish line that my brain was telling me was real, despite a big roadblock called heatstroke that rose up to stop me.

The danger, according to Gonzales, is the power the memory of our mental maps has over our rational decisions in risky and complex environments. "If things don't go according to the plan, revising such a robust model may be difficult. In an environment that has high objective hazards, the longer it takes to dislodge the imagined world in favour of the real one, the greater the risk. In nature, adaptation is important; the plan is not. It's a Zen thing. We must plan. But we must be able to let go of the plan, too."

To cope with adaptability in my ultrarunning adventures, I started to lean on my quit criteria after my Bryce Canyon misadventure. They help me stay true to my finishing goals when things get rough, they lay out the obvious roadblocks I might encounter in a long race, and they help me dislodge my imagined world, with a glorious finish line, and replace it with the real world where I must redraw my mental map and preserve myself based on my quit criteria.

During ultras, we put ourselves into conditions that mimic harsh survival circumstances in terms of geography, weather, exhaustion, and lingering pain. We set ourselves up for map/plan failure. Therefore, it's important to have quit criteria so that we can make our best *don't quit* choices based on all available intel. It's worked for me—on both sides of the coin.

CHAPTER 10

Pain vs. Injury

Deep into a three-week long-run training block, I'm awake at 4:30 a.m. Along the length of my shinbones, muscles are taut like pipes about to burst; the sensation is that of stretched fibres slowly tearing off the bone. It's a dull ripping ache that eases when I rotate my feet until my right big toe catches the sheets and, in angry retaliation, the calf above it constricts in a tight knot. I suck in a quick breath, throw back the covers and plunge my thumbs into the hard ball of flesh. My eyelids are pinched shut, but I see points of light.

Soles press the cold floor. Stiff ankles, the bones ringed with pain, render a walk that is anything but smooth. After an unsteady pee, I pause in the bathroom and, with a hand on the vanity to balance myself, stretch out my calves and wonder how I'll be able to run four hours from now. Slow lunging stretches tell me my quads and hamstrings are borderline. I should have taken in more water yesterday. I knew that but didn't do it.

Four and a half hours later, my watch syncs with unseen GPS signals emanating from satellites high above and somehow senses a heartbeat in the wrist it is strapped to. I push start and descend the path leading to the forest trail.

The first climb is utterly insignificant, but my calves ignite as if torched. Hard muscles are embodied as hard hurt: my mind's eye literally sees the contours of my solid calves as outlines of pain. The pain has shape. Rock-hard muscles in my feet have form; the ones atop my feet, to the outsides of my ankles, are like smooth oval stones, and the stones don't fit between the bones that surround them. It's a war between hardened muscle and unbending bone in my feet. They grind against each other with each footfall, and both surge in their own unique agony.

If I give in to this pain, tears will come to my eyes. I rarely let that happen. But the pain takes my breath away. I can't run far without oxygen, and the start of my 24-kilometre training run is a stilted run/walk. I grit my teeth and growl loudly to get some relief; from time to time, I cry out angrily and hope no one else is around. It hurts so much that if I had experienced this at any point in my life prior to ultrarunning, I would have hobbled home and sought medical help. I imagine most people would quit trying to run if they were exposed to this level of pain, but I've learned something about myself from pushing boundaries: this pain completely disappears after 5 to 6 kilometres. It will be gone in under an hour if I press on and endure it.

It's pain, not injury, and fifty minutes or so from now I will be climbing a trail with fresh legs, the same legs that have me near tears right now. With a jolt I will realize that, once again, the pain is gone. I will take a deep breath, smile, maybe laugh, and run off through the forest as though I had a perfect night's rest. My calves and feet will be loose and strong. If asked about my run later in the day, I will likely respond, "It was good, thanks. Joyful."

———

We have about three million pain receptors distributed externally and internally throughout our bodies that are triggered when skin, joints, muscles, or organs are damaged. "They transmit two types of pain to the brain. One is a sharp, instantaneous pain that signals your motor system to withdraw the hurting part of your body from the immediate stimulus to avoid further damage. The other is a duller background pain that tells your brain which area of the body has been injured and to temper its further use" (*The*

Brain: Big Bangs, Behaviors, and Beliefs, Rob DeSalle & Ian Tattersall).

Professional athletes, tradespeople with physical jobs, performers, and those with physical afflictions all live lives with dull background pain, or worse. For many, they have no choice but to exist with the ongoing agony; for others, like me at this time in my life, pain is a choice. I count myself fortunate in this regard, and though pain is something I can enter into or not partake of, I never take it lightly. In fact, my willing experience of pain leaves me in awe of those who live with inescapable pain. Knowing they cannot break free of their torment after less than an hour is a horrifying prospect for me. How they manage it, most of them gracefully, is a humbling mystery.

This is the context in which I want to talk about ultrarunning pain versus injury. There should be no bravado in the stories of pain that healthy ultrarunners share. A runner's pain is a choice and should be treated like nutrition and hydration—something to be figured out, planned for, and managed. Because there are three million little pain receptors waiting to do their thing, running far is going to incense many of them. It's the ultrarunner's job to learn the nuances of the body's raging response to running far, and deal with it. But runners should never boast about how bad it is for them; we can end our pain by ceasing to run. Others never choose their pain, nor can they escape it. It's important to note that and be respectful of it.

———

In the opening chapters, I told the story of how I went from not running at all to setting a goal to run 100 miles in a thirty-hour period before I turned sixty. I plucked the details of all the turning points and races from eleven years of my running journals. Looking back at the progression of distances and the race times always encourages to me. More instructional is looking back at the setbacks due to injury—especially when I'm freshly injured. New pains and injuries never fail to startle me, and they instantly cause me to think, *This is it. It's over.* But my journal helps me through the knee jerk oh-woe-is-me reaction by showing how pain and injury had their place in my long journey: often as negative occurrences that were overcome, and sometimes as blessings in disguise. And by looking back and tracking how I overcame those difficulties, I gain hope that I can do it again, just like I have hope—belief actually—at the start of each painful run that this too shall pass, and it does.

———

Injury: a time to stop, figure it out, realign, and manage future occurrences.

I clearly recall running the steep, steady climb from the valley park to the golf course on the ridge up above our Coquitlam home on a hot, sunny August 6, 2012. It was two weeks after I had run 20 kilometres for the first time—on a whim—and just over a month after I discovered I could run quite quickly for my age at my first Longest Day Road Race. I was wearing my Vibram Five Fingers minimalist slippers and moving up the slope with strong strides that delivered a solid workout. I remember how good that run felt. Shirt off, sun on wet skin, legs churning in measured bursts carrying me up the hill, building muscle.

Near the stairs that led up to our neighbourhood shopping centre, a sharp, instantaneous pain in the long bone connected to the second toe on my right foot hobbled me. I hopped to a stop at the stairs. I'd broken foot bones before—once with an inaccurately dropped concrete slab when I was about ten, and once in high school soccer—and I knew, on those stairs, I had a metatarsal fracture. The pinpoint pain was, without a doubt, signalling my motor system to withdraw my foot from the stimulus of that run. I limped through the shopping centre parking lot, feeling like a half-naked poser, a phony runner who'd just been exposed as a broken show-off. With much cursing and self-pity, I shuffled the 1.5 kilometres home, trying to land my right foot on its heel only. It was my first significant running injury, and it sent me into a panic. *Was running finished for me this quickly?*

Google. Google. Doctor visit. Google. Google. *I can fix this. Whew.*

Having figured out that mine was a common injury that would heal with time, I put my mind to work fixing the broken bone. I've been told I'm a bit strange in this regard. I tend not to view my ailments as problems that will heal on their own. Instead, I actively will my injuries to repair themselves. Apparently, the language I use with friends when I talk about my injury recovery strategies has revealed a "control freak" aspect in my personality. *Huh.*

Our spin bike and a tightly laced running shoe kept my legs moving over the next weeks, and my journal shows I ran again seven weeks later, on September 25, a reasonable time for bone fracture recovery. Looking back, it was inevitable that something was going to snap. I was just over a year out from going from zero running to training aggressively and racing fast, and I'd just given my feet a real pounding with their first 20-kilometre run in minimal footwear. At fifty years of age, I was lucky to have made it that far without something breaking apart.

Six months later, on February 10, 2013, I fractured the same bone in my left foot. Once again, the spin bike came in handy, and I discovered that lacing my foot tight in a skate wasn't so bad either. My journal shows I played hockey through that recovery period but didn't run again until March 17, another five-to-six-week bone-healing timeline.

How to keep the bones in my feet from repeated injury was suddenly the pressing question.

My problem required more than one solution. First, I had to step back and assess the context the injuries were occurring in. Thirty years of not running had left me with low bone density in my feet and legs, and one year of running wasn't long enough for my body to accommodate the ever-increasing beating I was laying on it. At the age of fifty, gaining bone density and getting stronger were going to take time, and I needed to take a more patient approach to increasing the foot pounding. Aggressive leaps forward in distance and intensity needed to be replaced by more gradual increases. The injuries convinced me that the time had come to make and monitor formal training plans.

Second, I needed to add restraint to my minimalist footwear strategy. While the Five Fingers and New Balance running "slippers" helped build foot muscles and improved my running form, they didn't offer enough protection on the rugged trails where the risk of injury was greater than the benefits they afforded me. I needed to be wiser with my footwear and less enthusiastic about being on-trend. I relented and finally bought myself a pair of real trail running shoes.

I also learned that I was susceptible to fractured foot bones because I had Morton's foot along with fifteen to twenty percent of the rest of humans whose second toe is longer than their big toe because their big toe metatarsal is shorter than average. (The percentage varies widely depending on ethnicity, population remoteness, etc.) This genetic trait made me vulnerable to a few things, including fractures of the metatarsals attached to the protruding digits, and nasty problems with toenails thrust into harm's way. And believe me, those long toes and their nails got smashed and bloodied on rocks and roots when I ran trails.

My solution to Morton's foot, or Morton's toe as it is also called, was to wear a trail runner one size too big. Some find this an imperfect solution because they like a tight-fitting shoe. I believed I benefitted from a looser fitting shoe that allowed my foot to shift inside it when the shoe bent the wrong way on a rock. Over the years I was repeatedly thankful when a shoe took a whacky twist off a rock and my foot didn't follow it all the way. Well aware that the "one size too big trail shoe debate" will forever remain un-settled, personal experience landed me squarely (well, more like sloppily) on the "big is best" side of that one.

The fracturing of my metatarsals ten years ago was injury, and I stopped running to heal appropriately. Since then, the density of my foot and leg bones has increased considerably, and I benefit from that every time I run. Footwear adjustments have also mini-mized subsequent injuries by better protecting, and making space for, my Morton's toes. Continuing to run through the torment of constantly stubbing those long toes is a choice I now make be-cause I know it is pain, not injury. Because it is bearable and tem-porary, I choose this pain, and I am certain that all runners must make similar choices regarding their own peculiar afflictions that arise from their particular body designs. To run far, repeatedly, is to live with some amount of pain, regardless of who we are.

———

With two weeks to go to my HomeRun100, I was enjoying an injury-free sixteen-week training block when a piercing pain blazed through my right ankle and I limped to a halt as though shot through the foot. It was new. It was bad. *What had I done?*

I could walk on it with some tenderness but I could not run without extreme pain. It hurt with rotation but not like a sprain. It was a mystery to Cindy who examined it several times, and it definitely *felt* like injury to me. It persisted day after day as my 100-miler approached, and I could do nothing more than walk 3 kilometres to the lake and 3 kilometres back. I considered calling the HomeRun100 weekend off. But I had more than ten friends coming to help with the event, some from great distances. As the days passed, I hotly debated the pain or injury diagnosis in my mind and with a few select running buddies. We were all left scratching our heads. It was disheartening to think my 100-miler could be thwarted by an out-of-nowhere ankle injury. I didn't even roll the thing!

I did not run a single stride during the two weeks prior to my HomeRun100: the ankle just hurt too much. During that time, I tested a few strategies for supporting the injury site and settled on a dual brace/wrap system cobbled together from pharmacy supplies.

I started my 100-mile weekend at 7 a.m. on a sunny Saturday morning. Without fanfare, Cindy took a starting line picture and Alley and I ran off down the hill. Ran—and the ankle held together. At the 60-kilometre Capra aid station stop, I changed runners and socks and the brace/wrap came off and didn't go back on. Over the course of those 100 miles, I experienced a lot of different pains, but nothing of note from that ankle.

That injury remains an oddity in my journal. Suddenly and forcefully there, then suddenly and quietly gone. Perhaps it was a dislocated foot bone? I had done that more than once before and solved those with forceful foot rolls. But no amount of foot rolling worked in that instance. It was a mystery.

The "oddity" taught me three things. One, to not pull the plug on a race I had worked hard for too soon, regardless of how bad something hurt or how unsolvable the problem first appeared. I had to hang tight to the belief that I would prevail. Second, to stop stressing about losing fitness during a planned taper. I ran zero kilometres for two weeks, and if anything, I benefitted more from all that rest on race day than any amount of running I would have done. Too many runners panic-train during their taper and end up exhausted at the start line. My little mystery injury saved me from that! Third, to test the injury at my A-race—I had nothing to lose by showing up and giving it a shot. Obviously, I knew I would quit if pain indicated that the injury was still present (remember those quit criteria), but I also needed to trust that if the symptoms of the injury mellowed or disappeared, I would be more than glad I hadn't abandoned my goal race. It taught me to show up, get out there, and get it done.

———

I dealt with many different aches, pains, and injuries in the ultra-running decade of my fifties. And regardless of whether they were pain or injury, I learned to address them by simply figuring them out. Once I got a handle on them, I then planned around them or managed them within my training plans. Once I knew it was not an injury, I learned to deal with pain as systematically as I dealt with fuelling and hydration and that helped put my pain in the right perspective.

I am grateful for the care I received: from Cindy, from massage therapists, from physiotherapists/acupuncturists, from my chiropractor, and from our family doctor. Every one of these people invested themselves in some way in my success. I'm also grateful for the little things that manage pain: rest, a good mattress, rollers, a tennis ball pressed into just the right pain point on my butt cheek to release the agony of a tight gluteus medius.

Finally, I'm grateful for my best friend, Glenn, who helps me keep my self-inflicted pain in perspective. I rarely finish a long run without thinking of him. His life with multiple sclerosis is a life of pain—exhausting pain. He does not have the option to get up in the morning and choose pain like I do. I know that if MS had not entered his life, today he would be stronger than me and more adventurous than me, because he has always been the one to lead our way into the wilderness. I run trails without him, and that's a sad thing. And yet he is always with me because when my pain comes, and I need a reason to keep putting one foot in front of the other, all I have to do is think about Glenn and how he, in great pain, puts one unsteady foot in front of the other, just to walk to the garden, and how he would give anything to be in voluntary pain with me up on a mountainside. How dare I quit in the face of pain? And so I embrace it and carry on for him.

In My Mind, Not My Legs

Who am I, what am I,
when I push myself this far?
And what is it that pulls me out here
to begin with?

CHAPTER 11

Mental Odds & Ends

Every run on my quest to go far in my fifties presented the opportunity to enhance mental strength and fortitude in the same way that every training run, if managed correctly, enhanced my physical power and endurance. Mental strength was built over time, just like leg strength.

Making the conscious choice to mentally engage each run was my entry point to begin working on my mental strength. The simplest way for me to achieve that was to run without audio, be that music, or podcasts, or books. I worked on being present during every run. Call it mindfulness, or being there, or any other self-help buzzword; for me it boiled down to mentally experiencing the run versus having just another running experience. I discovered there's a big difference between living vs. existing. Making the conscious choice to truly encounter each training run put my mind in a state where it was fully aware of all aspects of my body as it moved, and my surroundings as I moved through them.

The rhythmic sound of my trail shoes touching down and lifting off created a meditative beat that soothed my mind on the stressful days. *Choosing* to experience a run for an hour, mentally engaged with my footfalls and breathing, was the opposite of feeling like I had to bash out another hour of running to meet my quota. Engaged in this way, it didn't take long for me to crave being out on the trails for longer periods of time. That yearning then evolved into feeling like I was being pulled out on my trail runs.

The sense of being drawn into the mountains and finding joy in the experience was the state of mind I sought to centre myself on during my hard training days, and when I was deep in the punishing places of an ultramarathon. A mind trained to engage with the flow of my strides through the forest, and the landing of my feet on uneven ground, became a mind that could keep my feet moving when my legs wanted to give up.

———

At the end of my training block for the 2022 Squamish50/50, I put the invitation out to runners in the Saturday morning Capra Trail Running Club to join me on a DeBeck's Hill climb after the group run. I'd run 10 kilometres before getting to Capra that morning, the group added another 12 kilometres, and I wanted to throw tired legs at one last 500-metre climb and descent before starting to taper toward the race.

A Fabio-haired newcomer named Chase Martini was up for another climb and joined me. It was a hot day. I was, to put it mildly, wrecked and ready to recover. After my 22 morning kilometres I did not move up that hill with purpose. It was ugly. It was the first time that year that I had to stop, numerous times, with hands on knees, to rest and pull myself together for the next vertical push. I was embarrassed, but thankfully Chase was a bit pooped too, and very gracious about my rest stops and huffing and puffing.

Two-thirds of the way up, we got to the final junction before the single trail to the top. "Well, Chase," I wheezed, "carry on to the top, or turn this show around and head down to your car?"

"Your choice," he replied. The look on Chase's face said he'd accept heading back to the car. Or perhaps it conveyed his concern that the tired old guy he was climbing with might keel over.

"If we go down now, we aren't ultrarunners," I said after fully catching my breath.

"How's that?"

"They say you know you're an ultrarunner when you get to

a junction, all pooped out, and you chose the longer, harder way home. Because that's when the mental training takes over."

We stood in the cool of the trees for a while. In previous years I would have happily headed down at that point, confident enough in my exhaustion to justify that I'd done enough for the day. But 2022 was the year of my big mileage ultramarathons. I was training differently and taking a purposeful approach to building mental strength as much as leg strength. That morning, two-thirds up that heat-baked mountain, was one of those tiny *don't quit* moments that all added up to something real when I needed it later.

"Up we go," I said, drawing a deep breath and turning to address the incline. I could feel my brain shift gears, like dropping the Jeep into 4-low.

I can't remember if Chase muttered anything at that point, but I sensed he was good to go.

The next section was steep. I recall how we faltered a bit before we both started to get stronger. At the top, sweat-soaked, with hands on hips as we looked to the peaks of the Tantalus Range to the west, we were all smiles as our laboured breathing subsided. I also recall how we ran all the trails from the top down to the car, 5 kilometres nonstop. That was impressive, given our poor performance on the climb. When we parted, I could tell Chase was pleased with how he'd elevated his game that day. I, too, was happy with our strong finish—physical and mental. My extra end-of-training-day climbs were paying off; it was good to have that last mental *don't quit* win heading toward my second 50/50 attempt. It proved to me that when my tank felt empty, I still had more if I dug for it.

Five months later, Chase became a full-fledged ultrarunner when he completed the Deception Pass 50K in Washington State, his first ultra-race. It takes hard training choices to get there, and he continued to make those choices for himself, bagging his second ultra, the difficult Diez Vistas 50K, soon after.

———

Without a doubt, being *ready* is the one thing I strive for as my pre-race taper draws to a close and the starting corral gets nearer. So, what does being *ready* mean?

For me, the key element is trust. I trust that I've executed the correct training plan and that I'm physically prepared. I trust that my race-day plan is good enough to keep me from sabotaging my own race through dumb decisions or neglected actions. I trust that my crew will do the things we planned for and be imaginative when obstacles arise. I trust that barring the unexpected arrival of any dangerous quit conditions I will have the mental fortitude— honed by training—to not quit even when I'm at my lowest. When I'm comfortable with all of this … I am ready.

Knowing I am ready sets my expectations, convictions, and determination to game mode. That heightened sense of purpose doesn't show up by chance—it's created. Most of all, being ready exists in my mind, not my legs.

———

Mantra is "support for the mind." Given how much time can be spent training our bodies to withstand the difficulties of an ultramarathon, it follows that attention should be given to propping up our minds through the difficult hours as well.

For me, mantras are the embodiment of mental readiness and a statement of purpose that encompasses what needs to be achieved in the moment. (Wow, I just typed that off the top of my head after a few sips of Baileys while half-watching a hockey game. Must experiment with this more, but I digress.)

My mantras come in all shapes and sizes. Most are personal enough to not be readily understood by others. A good example is the mantra I used for my 2017 Squamish50-Miler: *I have to run home*. It ranks as one of my most powerful motivators, used only once to great effect—and it encompassed so much that day. The story behind the mantra is that Cindy and I took possession of our first condo in Squamish the week before the race, and the condo was 400 metres from the Squamish50 finish line. We were fulfilling a dream by moving part-time to Squamish—getting our pre-retirement foot in the door—and *I have to run home* welled up as a solid statement of purpose. Come what may, I was determined to run back to our new home, our new life. There was a desperation and urgency and pleasure to that one that kept me moving all day. It inspired me to leave it all out there in a fight for a finish line and a future, both ensconced in the safety that home brings. There was great strength in that mantra.

Some mantras are a gift. Alley, the opening pacer on my HomeRun100, gave me my mantra for that day, *He believed he could do it. And he did it.* The phrase played repeatedly in my head through the hardest segments of that event. Stating the past tense, *And he did it,* as a preordained outcome, in the present, encompassed what I needed to achieve in the moment. Telling myself that I already owned the finish was an elixir during my darkest hours. Words have power in my mind, so I use them.

I was embarrassed to share the mantra I used for my second attempt at the Squamish50/50 in August 2022 because I was afraid it sounded cocky: *I finished 100 miles.* But for me, it encompassed everything I mentally needed to attempt what would ultimately be a harder challenge than my HomeRun100. I needed to keep telling myself that I had already made it through a thirty-hour 100-miler four months earlier, and because of that, I had the strength to take on the more daunting ascents, descents, heat, and nighttime stop/start of the 50/50. There was no bragging in that mantra. Instead, it was an indisputable statement of fact that I could cling to—the lifeline my mind latched onto to gain mental confidence. It was my runner's prayer.

I don't recall ever using the same mantra twice. For me they are time sensitive. They tend not to arise during training. They sometimes aren't solidified for me until early in a race. Alley's mantra gift, given when my race was already underway, is an example of that. In life, we don't always have the important words sorted out until it's time to say them with their context precisely established. Mantras are as fleeting as the few hours I use them. Significantly there in context, and then forever gone.

If using mantras makes sense to you, you will figure out what your mantras need to be for the situations in which you use them. If using mantras makes zero sense to you, try a bit of Baileys and flip on a hockey game. Perhaps you too will achieve clarity ... or maybe not.

———

I'm going to top off this little pile of mental odds and ends with a cautionary note about the day after you cross the finish line. The morning you wake up and no longer have an audacious goal bearing down on you. The day when all you can remember about the race is that it happened so fast that you weren't able to grasp the details, and now ... it's over.

It's really "done"—the word I used to sum up my HomeRun100 finish.

The sixteen-week training block your life was organized around is history.

All the mental preparation is spent.

Race day, and all the nerves, pain, joys, panic, thrills, losses, and small hourly victories that got packed into that day, or days, abruptly ended when you crossed the finish line or handed in your bib with a DNF.

It's all over.

And all the details of what happened on race day, and how

those details spun out of the months and years of training that preceded them, will not be unpacked until weeks and months later when memories of the race resurface through conversations or reading or seeing something online or on TV.

Race day, for me, literally pops back up, piece by piece, like a handful of submerged tub toys after initially vanishing beneath the bubbles for a time.

The abruptness of it being over takes a mental toll. I have experienced some motivational floundering and a sense of being lost when the lengthy and intense preparation for an ultra came to a sudden end and a purposeless vacuum took its place.

It was not a crisis, but it was a form of loss that I came to understand, along with the realization that I had to deal with it and not become listless or grumpy. No one wants to hear an ultrarunner mope about the fact that they have nothing to do three days after everyone celebrated their big finish with them. Some friends (and definitely relatives) don't have kind ways of saying, "Get a life."

The end of your big race may yield rest for your legs, but don't be surprised if it agitates your mind.

Runners need to know this and be prepared for it. And if you're prone to the post-race letdown like I am, a simple solution is to have the next interesting item on your agenda planned: the next family event, the next holiday, the next work or personal project you're keen on, and yes, maybe even your next race. Don't finish to nothing. End with something waiting on your to-do list. Then, enjoy your race-day memories as they slowly resurface over time.

You *can* overcome the post-race blues. Heck, you just ran an ultra!

CHAPTER 12

Unconscious Competent

In the howl of the wind and the rustle of cascading fir and cedar twigs, I heard the explosive pop-crack of a tree trunk to my left. The corner of my eye caught dark bark flying outward, driven by an expanding ball of yellow-tan splinters—the heartwood of the hundred-foot tree. As if in agony, the trunk twisted and leaned above the shatter point, and the monstrous weight of it began descending through the trees with me in its fall line.

The terrain ascended to my right. I recall the chaos of clawing up the embankment and the hardness of the stones and roots I threw myself upon, behind the massive stump I scrambled toward.

Boughs rained down. Wind roared. So much wood snapped above me. The stricken monster did not land. I looked up to see it momentarily suspended in a knotted tangle of other trees. The air was a maelstrom of needles and sticks and grit.

Back on the trail again, I sprinted uphill, desperate to get over the ridge and away from the northern gale that had struck without notice minutes before. *On the other side, I'll be sheltered.* Adrenaline powered long strides to the crest of the trail, and once over it, I ran a long way into the still forest. Not a branch moved there, although the sound of the wind tearing over the hilltop, deflected over these trees, still surrounded me.

When I finally stopped to catch my breath, the first thing I noticed was the dislocated pinky on my left hand. Knowing what to do from hockey locker rooms past, and knowing I had to act fast or not act at all, I grabbed it, gave it a sharp pull, and felt it realign—the numbing effect of my shock a useful anesthetic. My hands were all dirt and blood. Further investigation revealed gashes in my knees and shins with goose egg bumps here and there where legs and arms had collided with rock and root.

In an instant, the forest became a deadly place. In that instant, my conscious mind was not in charge of the actions I took to flee a specific threat. As I ran home, quite shaken, I had enough wits about me to marvel at how my unconscious mind had ignored inevitable cuts and bruises in its attempt to save the body it inhabited. No weighing of pros and cons took place when the beast descended on me; logical and emotional analysis were subservient to rapid-fire instructions that caused my body to act in a split second.

Who, or what, did that?

———

At a Capra Trail Running Club Halloween event, I discovered that I could run in the dark with a bucket on my head. The bucket had eyeholes—similar in size and alignment to the eyeholes in a Stormtrooper's helmet—and they were covered with a black see-through fabric. Two funny friends, Solana Green and Catherine Fleming, constructed three quite functional bucket headpieces. Dressed alike, our trio was a hit.

With bucket on, I stumbled around the uneven ground at the trailhead of the nighttime scavenger hunt run that Solana had engineered. Concerned that I was headed for a bad fall, I came to the quick conclusion that I'd have to ditch the headpiece, and said so.

"No way!" the skeletons, cowboys, ladybug, cows in running tights, and supersized green leaf chimed, along with a lot of laughter. Then someone jokingly told me to lead the way. Probably the overly talkative mime.

The energy of the group was contagious, so I aimed my hand-held headlamp down the trail and started to run just to be silly—

fully anticipating a quick trip, fall, and some goodhearted cheering.

Quite the opposite happened: I ran ahead at reasonable speed—no problem.

Twenty-or-so partygoers followed, as did big laughter, and from the hoots behind me I could tell that Solana and Catherine were running easily with their buckets on too. My notion to dump the bucket axed, I unsuspectingly led the menagerie to a horrific encounter with Stephen Kings's the Grady sisters, serving blood red shooters at a trail intersection in the coal-black woods. Who else but volunteer phenoms, Suzanne and Annie. Black night. Bucket on. Booze in. We went running in the woods.

Tunnel vision, on a dark trail with wavering light, worked just fine. I could run at speed, and I didn't take the bucket off for the next two hours of running, climbing, and descending, although the steeper descents demanded a slower, more cautious approach.

How the heck did all that work?

With a little thought, most runners should be able to explain how I was able to run (easily) with my view restricted to only that which lay down the trail a ways in front of me. That's where we always look when we run! I initially stumbled when I walked because we tend to look at the ground much closer to our feet when we walk—and that's where my vision was restricted. I couldn't see anything down there with the bucket on. Whenever the group came to a stop, we three running bucket-heads stumbled around, which added to the comedy of the outing. We could literally run but not walk.

Perhaps the better question is why, when someone shouted for me to lead, did I instinctively believe that I could just start running on an uneven forest trail loaded with natural tripping hazards, with a bucket on my head?

Who, or what, made the calm unconscious decision that I could do it, and why didn't I hesitate?

———

Many moons ago, when I was a young lad at university, I was introduced to a learning model that's been useful throughout my life. A quick search of the web tells me the model is ubiquitous and goes by many names nowadays. I will call it the Unconscious Competent Learning Model and I hope that title comes close to what my textbooks called it in the early 80s.

It's a simple tiered structure.

The bottom level is the unconscious incompetent. This was me in my early thirties in relation to playing hockey. Having not played an organized game since grade seven, I had the urge to play hockey as an adult. Some friends encouraged me to purchase the gear and I stepped back on the ice with them. What a thrill! I shuttled around the rink, made some passes, discovered I could still skate well enough to keep up, and potted a goal off a perfect pass from a friend. I had so much fun! And in my exuberance, I was blissfully unaware of how bad a player I was. I was totally unconscious of my incompetence for the first few games, all the while buoyed up by everyone who encouraged me to keep going and "Just play with heart!"

The fun ended when I moved one tier up on the model and became a conscious incompetent player, plunking myself down on the bench at the end of each shift with a heaviness I hadn't experienced early on. "Sorry about the bad pass, man." "Sorry about losing it in the corner, guys." "Sorry for deflecting the puck into our net." "Sorry. Sorry. Sorry." As the novelty of being back on the ice wore off, the blinders came off, too, and it became obvious to me that compared to everyone else, I sucked. Having started after Christmas, the first season mercifully ended soon after I awoke to my poor play. I then did what any self-respecting incompetent would do: I signed up for a summer hockey school league. Heaven forbid I let incompetence stand in the way of having fun.

Hockey school ushered me up to the third tier of learning. That was where the work of athletic improvement began and where I slowly became a conscious competent, skating on the thin ice where conscious willfulness turned into physical performance with incompetence still trying to pull me down from below. In many aspects of our physical lives, whether with sports or physical job skills, we remain at the conscious competent level forever. We have to think a lot about the trickier physical actions we execute.

In sport, we immediately know who the top tier unconscious competent is: they are the elite athlete who has eyes in the back of their head, or the ability to see the play, or they appear to make the play slow down, and they consistently exhibit the ability to move at speed while executing maneuvers the rest of us can only dream about.

Oddly enough, it's in our mundane daily lives where the rest of us find our unconscious competent selves. How else do we explain putting our hands back at the ten and two o'clock positions on the steering wheel after fiddling with our seatbelts, adjusting the AC and radio and opening our pop while cruising around a corner in heavy traffic going 60 miles per hour, all the while carrying on a conversation? The unconscious competent driver in most of us keeps us in our lane and handles the curve while our eyes dart everywhere else until our conscious brain clicks back on and questions how we got to that place on the highway—and we trust ourselves to do that without hesitation—just like I trusted myself to run down the trail with a bucket on my head. Something inside me knew it could be done based on the tiered learning my brain had amassed over repeated running experiences.

I think this is why trail running appeals to me so much at my late age. It gives me athletic moments of pure joy when my unconscious competence is in play. I can pass through miles of technical terrain without having *thought* about how to do it, and it's in those long periods in the woods and on the hills that I truly internalize the run. I *am* nature as I move along the trails, my choices guided by an unconscious competency that looks ahead down the trail and has all my footfalls figured out for the 10 metres of ground I'm not even looking at anymore. It's a feeling of doing something I am built to do—well.

———

As the sweeper for the Saturday morning Capra Trail Running Club, I regularly meet people who are transitioning through the lower levels of the unconscious competent learning model in their running lives. I see it right away on the downhills as they stop and think about where each foot is going to land, and I encourage them to not get down on themselves because others are flying down the slope and disappearing into the woods below; it takes time and repetition for competence to become unconscious.

"Enjoy the process," I tell them. "Experience the run for what it is. Don't overthink. Instead, relax and try to move with the terrain. There's something ancient inside you that knows the best way down the hill. Learn to let it do the work. The joy will come."

Recognizing which level you're at, on the scale from unconscious incompetent to unconscious competent, offers perspective on your feelings and frustrations in new sporting endeavours and in other areas of your life. For me, acknowledging which of the two middle levels I'm at has been of great help in my alpine adventures of recent years. I know I am a conscious incompetent when I'm up against a scramble with significant exposure. The benefit of knowing that is I can better judge when I need to stop and ask my hiking partners for help. I'm old enough now to know there's no shame in saying, "I don't know how to do this safely." Experience has taught me that if I surround myself with good people, they will help when help is needed. Being conscious of when I'm in a position of incompetence is knowing when not to take a risk without help.

The other benefit of recognizing which level of competence you're functioning at is the assistance that knowledge can render in helping you sort out if you're physically or mentally exhausted during training. I can absolutely guarantee that someone who runs road marathons, but who has never run trail before, will be drop dead pooped after their first 13-kilometre Capra Saturday trail run—not from physical exhaustion, but mental exhaustion. It will manifest as physical exhaustion, but I will have seen the intensity in their eyes and witnessed their clenched jaw and the concentration on their face as they navigated the uneven ground and worried about the grip of their runners on the angled granite.

On their smartwatch, that run will be one of the slowest of their year, but their brains will have gone a million miles an hour. This is important for new trail runners to understand because their exhaustion is not an indication that they're suddenly unfit; it's an indication that the navigational part of their brain is inexperienced when it comes to all the obstacles a forest throws at people moving quickly through it. Concentrating on foot placement is tiring; running fast through the woods without thinking about it is joy. New trail runners don't necessarily have to get more fit to be less worn out, just more competent.

Physical activity at the conscious incompetent level is the most exhausting of all. Understanding this is the key to battling through tiredness to build physical and mental strength during training. Pushing a tired mind forward to improve the fitness of the legs early in training can result in a stronger mind moving tired legs forward at the end of an ultra. The trick is to know whether you're feeling mental or physical exhaustion. Learning to *experience the run* can help build this differentiated awareness.

Finally, I don't think we can ever boast that we've attained the unconscious competent level in the athletic things we do. It's OK to look back and see evidence of it happening, and it's OK to trust when it is happening (because chances are we aren't even aware of it...*duh, it's called unconscious*), but I wouldn't stand at the top of a technical descent and throw caution to the wind and then race down believing my unconscious ninja skills will kick in. Luke switched off his targeting computer and used the Force, that's true, but that was a movie. My suggestion is that we discover our unconscious competence in hindsight. If we pursue a physical activity long enough, the unconscious competent in us will turn on, and we will learn to trust it. Then, when we reflect on how the deep functioning of our mind unleashed us to move and flow, I hope our joy will be accompanied by gratitude for how wondrous we are.

———

And speaking of hindsight, what about that split-second escape I had from the falling tree? Looking back, who, or what guided me through that?

I think it's safe to say the unconscious competent in me acted that day, and the experience of being guided by my innate survival mechanisms had a profound impact. It was one of those extraordinary life events when I encountered *what I was*, rather than *who I was*, as my archaic mind took control and drove me to act on instinct; and then, having submerged to the depth of my reptilian brain, I resurfaced to emotion, and finally, once I was clear of the danger, I elevated back to my cerebral sapiens day-to-day realm of thought and reflection. A unique mental descent and return through the stacked layers built over millions of years. Something to mull over on long runs in the woods.

Some will say, "What about God, or what about the Universe? Could they not have moved you to safety?"

And I will reply, "That's a good trail topic. I look forward to seeing you out there. We can chat!"

CHAPTER 13

Why Did I Do It?

"There's simply no way to finish an ultramarathon without giving yourself up to it entirely—no shortcuts or paths of least resistance to follow. If you want to run an ultra, you have to be willing to train and prepare like never before. Few people have the discipline or patience for this. For some of us, ultrarunning is the perfect antidote to the madness of everyday living. Few feelings in life make more sense than placing one foot in front of the other and repeating, over and over again.

"There are other compelling factors. Chiefly, it really hurts. Life is easy, so why do something excruciatingly hard? Because life is easy. And therein lies the conflicted magic of ultrarunning. Some people get this, but most don't. In a world that's become obsessed with convenience and ease, ultrarunning provides some-thing gruelling and uncertain. You reach the halfway point and things get really interesting."
—Dean Karnazes, "The Internal Workings of an Ultrarunner,"
  UltraRunning Magazine, Nov 2020

"There are things to learn about yourself that can only be dis-covered when you walk up to the borderline of your comfort zone and then bravely step over that line into the unknown."
—Cory Reese, "Where the Roads Don't Go,"
  UltraRunning Magazine, Nov 2020

———

For the first five years that I ran ultras, I believed I did it because they were hard, *boom*, full stop, that was the reason.

My reasoning was founded on the words J.F. Kennedy spoke at Rice University to cold war America in 1962, the year I was born: "We choose to go to the moon … and do the other things, not because they are easy, but because they are hard."

Fascinated since childhood by the space program, and a reader of at least one Mercury/Gemini/Apollo memoir or engineering book a year, I continue to be inspired by individuals and organizations that strive to achieve the seemingly impossible. It was easy for me to adopt Kennedy's challenge as my life's mantra (without the moon part, of course).

Doing things because they were hard made sense as the *why* for many things I did in my life, from choosing to be a creative entrepreneur rather than a maintainer, to choosing to lead more than follow, to testing my own beliefs, to choosing to go far after I stumbled into trail running in my early fifties. Doing things just because they were hard, and therefore challenging, made sense until I started to notice, in my late fifties, that I wasn't *choosing* to run farther and farther distances, I was *being pulled* to run them. And suddenly, *because it is hard* wasn't big enough to encompass the pull I was experiencing in my running life.

Then along came 2020 and the pandemic apple cart upset and a book and a magazine that simultaneously arrived at my reading chair that fall: David Roberts' *Limits of the Known,* and the November 2020 edition of *UltraRunning Magazine (UR).*

Limits of the Known is mountaineer and adventurer David Roberts' final book, written when he was in the clutch of cancer and searching to articulate the *why* behind his repeated choices to risk his life, the lives of others, and his relationships, in his attempts to achieve the impossible. A non-stop read, I started to see hints of what could potentially be my own broader personal *why* in Roberts's exposition of the various motivators he explored as his *raisons d'être* before he finally settled on one *why* that drove him to his mountain summits.

In the November 2020 pandemic issue of *UR*, longtime contributors were asked, in the soul-searching absence of ultraraces and the loss of runner identity associated with a summer of race cancellations, "Why do we run ultras?" Having just finished Roberts' book, it was fascinating to see the contributors to *UR* land on every theory Roberts espoused about why he pushed his limits at high altitude. I found the articles of such value that my heavily underlined copy of that edition has its own special place on my running bookshelf.

Taken together, *Limits of the Known* became the flame beneath the *UR* crucible that held the elements of what now forms my *why*.

––––

For Christmas, 1998, my brother-in-law Gerald VanDyck gave me the book *Into Thin Air* by Jon Krakauer, the story of the 1996 disaster on Everest. I recall staying up way too late reading it on a business trip to Orlando, Florida. Smart, strong people chose to violate all their quit criteria and not abandon the hard climb, and in turn, many tragically perished on their descent. "Why did we risk so much to achieve something of so little value?" was the question I heard in Krakauer's traumatic recounting of risky decisions made and lives lost. Unfortunately, he poured his story out so soon after his ordeal that he couldn't articulate the answer. I'm not sure he ever has.

That book set me on a path to reading at least one mountaineering book each year since, and it ultimately set me on the path to Everest Base Camp with Cindy and Jeanette in 2015. I had to see and touch what I was reading about in the same way that I have seen and touched a number of the Apollo command modules that journeyed to the moon. (Set off a museum alarm doing my *touching history* thing once too!)

Over the years, I read the mountaineering classics: Maurice Herzog's *Annapurna*, Sir Edmund Hillary's *High Adventure*, Reinhold Messner's *Everest, Expedition to the Ultimate*, Sir Christopher Bonington's numerous books, Wade Davis's *Into The Silence* (the best recounting of George Mallory's expeditions one can find), and many more besides. I think for a while Cindy worried I might be concealing a secret plan to disappear and climb a Himalayan peak. Not to worry, it turned out that becoming an ultrarunner would be enough, and of course, getting to Everest Base Camp with her—in hindsight, astounding, given that neither of those physical achievements were on the radar for me, the portly and unhealthy international business traveller reading *Into Thin Air*, back in the late 90s.

In 2020, and with bookshelves of mountaineering and spaceflight memoirs as the backdrop, I read Roberts' *Limits of the Known*. In it, I saw him struggle to answer his *why* by looking to the words of the adventurers who had gone before him—the words I, too, had read over the years. And as one would expect, Roberts began with first legend of Everest, George Mallory, lost on the North Ridge in June 1924 (and found and buried by Conrad Anker in June 1999).

Exploring Mallory's *why*, Roberts writes, "The temptation … is to divine some higher purpose served by all those journeys into the wilderness. Mallory … in an essay published in the *Alpine Journal* in 1918 [wrote]: 'Have we vanquished an enemy? None but ourselves.' This quasi-mystical affirmation evolved over subsequent decades into the claim that the reward for flirting with death in the pursuit of summits was the discovery of self. Reinhold Messner was particularly addicted to this formula."

Though not a fan of the self-absorbed Messner, I have questioned if my choice to pursue ultrarunning all the way to the 100-mile distance in my fifties was to discover *myself* in some Malloryesque kind of way. Maybe so. The journey was, without doubt, the embodiment of my mid-life crisis. I didn't get a motorcycle or hair implants; instead, I ran trails—really far. Was that my way of vanquishing the enemy of my old age? Was I going on my journeys into the wilderness to find my inner Edmund Hillary, or Chris Bonington, or Neil Armstrong while I still had the energy to emulate them in some way?

No, I'm not convinced I trained and struggled to go 100 miles to find my inner explorer self. Even though I did become an explorer, in my own small way. I'm not convinced either that the different physiological me discovered at 80 kilometres, and the different mental me at 120 kilometres, constitute the *self* Mallory and Messner were searching for when they pushed their limits to find themselves in some esoteric sense.

Roberts, likewise, writes, "I remain deeply skeptical about the facile proposition that through the trials of extreme adventure we learn the bedrock truths about ourselves." And with that he concludes that the *why* behind his pursuit of difficult objectives was not to find himself. And I agree.

———

Having set aside the search for *self* as the driver behind his mountaineering exploits, Roberts then surprises us with what he says next. "Perhaps joy is the reward. Mallory said as much, in a less well-known quote about the purpose of ascent: 'What we get from this adventure is just sheer joy. And joy is, after all, the end of life.'"

Joy? Seriously? The ultimate goal of all the hardships Mallory endured in the Himalaya was joy? On the surface, that seems crazy as my motivation for running ultras. Flaming, freezing, and chafing for joy?

Then, if I let it steep a bit … maybe?

Cory Reese, in his November 2020 *UR* article, "Where the Roads Don't Go," supports the notion of joy as he reflects on seeing a spectacular sunrise at the end of a hard night on a desert ultra: "Ultramarathons give you a chance to stand in a place like this where the roads don't go. You have a deeper appreciation for moments like this because you have to earn them. Now that was worth running 100 miles for."

I can whole heartedly relate to that. When I take into account the brief agony of a DNF, I have to acknowledge that it was nothing compared to all the moments of joy along the thousands of kilometres of training trails that got me there. So many of those training runs contained rarefied experiences with nature, and people, and myself, where I simply had to exclaim, like Reese, "Now that was worth running for!"

Those moments were joyful.

In a stitched-together set of quotes from Amy Rusiecki's November 2020 *UR* article, "Why Run Ultras?" she says, "I'm trying to boil a million memories and feelings into a handful of coherent words. I remember my celebration, perhaps even disbelief, when I've achieved a major goal or PR, especially when it's the culmination of months or years of training and focus. There's no way to describe it to someone who hasn't participated and felt those same emotions. Is there any way to relate the teary-eyed emotions as I crossed the finish line of my first 50-miler, exhausted yet amazed at accomplishing something I believed was beyond my capabilities? There are few words to truly describe these feelings, emotions and sights."

Perhaps "joy" is one of those words?

And then I sit back and reflect, and I find myself concluding that although joy does indeed express what I derive from ultrarunning, the attainment of joy isn't *why* I do it. I don't find myself searching for joy when I take my first steps on a trail run, in the same way that I don't find myself searching for who I am when I'm on the trail either.

My passion to put in the hard work, absorb failure, and carry on as an ultrarunner is not about a search, it is more of a response to a pull. And if that's true, what is pulling me? And what is it pulling me toward?

Why, as it got harder and harder, did I choose to continue to keep my sights set on completing a 100-miler by the time I turned sixty? What drew me there?

———

After exploring joy as the *why* behind his adventures, David Roberts, in *Limits of the Known*, dismisses joy as too subjective and moves to an objective cause: "we are wired to do hard things," he concludes; "we are wired for adventure."

What makes this angle interesting is that Roberts uses the word "adventure" in the context of its original meaning: to adventure is to risk. This risk, to him, is the romantic notion that informs the *why* he settles upon.

"If my romantic notion has any merit, then it would recast 'adventure' not as some exploit we choose to pursue, but as the response to an instinct embedded in our genes. It would help me understand why it's so hard to articulate what drove me to adventure and what it gave me in the end." Replace the word "adventure" in his quote with the word "risk," and you suddenly see Roberts find the answer to why he chose to imperil himself, his fellow climbers, and the most important relationships in his life for the sake of mountaintops. To paraphrase: Roberts' romantic notion would recast risk as the response to an instinct embedded in our genes.

It is a startling conclusion to me. In his final book, Roberts states that he risked it all because he was wired for adventure. I wrestle with that. It's like Roberts lets himself off the hook by declaring he didn't have a choice to risk lives and relationships when he climbed—his genetics drove him to it.

I don't buy this conclusion completely … it's missing something.

Are all humans wired for the risks Roberts took in his life? Are all humans born to run? If so, shouldn't the world look a whole lot different? Roberts is a wonderful exception to the human standard—that's why his books are so riveting. We read them wide-eyed with mouths agape because we can't believe what he achieved and lived to tell us about. Likewise, it is my experience that I am an oddball as an ultrarunner at my age. I don't think I am wired for risky adventure any more than all those people around me who could care less about running up their driveway or climbing onto anything other than their sofa. I wasn't wired to complete a 100-mile run, even though I agree with author Christopher McDougall that my body was *Born To Run*. I chose to do it. My genes didn't make the call. Nor do I think that they suddenly woke up to who they were supposed to make me when I turned fifty.

I recall digging through my glove and toque drawer in the closet by our front door early one winter morning, in search of a warmer pair of mitts for a 30-kilometre training run, when Cindy arrived home from a night shift. She asked me if I really wanted to go outside right then and gave an unfavourable report of her hazardous drive home.

"I'm really up for this one today," was my reply. I was excited to go. I was feeling a pull to get out that door from the moment I woke up.

It was cold and icy outside. I knew the effort was going to be much harder than a typical training run in good weather. I knew I risked injury in those conditions, and yet I was primed to get going.

What pulled me?

It certainly wasn't genetics, because for the fifty-three years prior to running ultras I never had any such desires.

———

This is the big question. What pulls me to keep cranking out the long miles on the trails if it's not to find myself, or experience joy, or because I'm somehow wired for adventure?

For me, the pivotal article in the November 2020 issue of *UR* is Gary Cantrell's "Evolution." His thesis makes the most sense to me, and his words form the foundation on which I finally set my *why*.

"We are a collection of systems that were designed with the assumption of physical activity. From bone density to mental health, every part of our makeup relies on activity to keep it operating at an optimal level. Why then, did we not develop a craving for exercise? Because for most of our history as a species, and all the species that came before us, physical activity was guaranteed."

Stop for a moment and let that soak in. Maybe read it again. For most of our history, physical activity was guaranteed.

... OK, let's let Gary continue.

"We did not need to evolve a craving for activity. Rather, we evolved fatigue to keep us from expending all of our energy resources. We evolved quitting (an adaptation common to all animals) to prevent us from burning up all our resources in a pursuit that is fruitless. We evolved the propensity to rest. We evolved the drive to find 'an easier way.'"

Wow. Stack that up against "we are wired for adventure" and the mind starts churning.

"All of these were positive adaptations, until we became too successful with the last one. We gain weight as a reserve against famines that never come. Rather than spur us to get more physically active, we retreat from discomfort into a more sedentary lifestyle. Physicians know that the best treatment for a variety of ailments is simple exercise. But they do not prescribe it. Why? Because people will not do it."

Maybe that's because people aren't wired for adventure?

Gary brings the discussion into his world—the ultrarunners' world. "Whatever value we ascribe to the race ... it is the training that is the real value. Having a training plan, keeping a log, and breaking ourselves loose from the inertia that keeps us on the sofa—that's the value of having goals. Until the hunter-gatherer lifestyle returns, we need to provide our own impetus to get the most valuable nutrient of all: physical activity."

———

We are not wired for adventure. Instead, we are wired for resting.

When I stumbled upon this unexpected epiphany in 2020, I compiled all the quotes that got me there and filed them. It was a watershed moment in my thinking.

And why are we wired for resting?

It's because of *what we are* at our two-million-year-old core: hunters, gatherers, scavengers, moving, fleeing, chasing. This leads me to infer that when we move and flee and chase to the extent that our running ancestors did, and to the upper limits our bodies are designed for, our unconscious minds become energized by a reconnection to the deep roots of what we physically are: a species of communal endurance runners/hunters/survivors.

Jason Koop, in his article "Reconnect With Your Why" (*UR*, Nov 2020), lends further perspective to this connection between extreme human activities and our historic dependence on community. "Ultrarunners are kindred spirits. For we all know what it's like to suffer, and we all know what it's like to persevere. Some of our best friendships are made trailside. These friendships are forged in footsteps and they feel real, substantive, and everlasting. It is more to us than just a sport; it is a deep and meaningful connection with something divine and sacred. An ultramarathon may be difficult, but it always takes us to a place unlike any other."

Is this another way of saying that when ultrarunners suffer and persevere together, they bond in a reawakening to what they are at their core—a collection of systems designed with the assumption of communal physical activity intended to overcome suffering, and to persevere, in order to survive? And if this is a legitimate theory of what we are as beings of flesh and bone, why does Koop use metaphysical words like divine and sacred to describe the ultrarunner's experience of what they are?

My response is that when an ultrarunner, or adventurer, crosses the experiential line where their being senses that they are fulfilling, through difficult physical activities, what they are designed to be, the cognitive jolt of the soul remembering that ancient connection feels like a mystical experience—sacred and divine. The use of metaphysical or spiritual terminology is how humans have expressed those enlightened moments since abstract thought first became part of our toolset. To me, this is similar to the revelation a forest bather experiences when they awaken to the notion that they *are* nature, not a separate being *in* nature. For many people, this subtle change in perception crashes on them as an earth-shattering moment of enlightenment, and many dub it a spiritual experience because they simply have no other way to describe it.

Does a similar subtle change in the perception of *what we are* occur through the experience of adventuring and ultrarunning? Is my mind's awareness of that (at unconscious levels, I presume) the *why* behind why I run ultras, and the *what* that pulls me out the door to run a trail, or climb a hill, that does not, for any arguable reason, need to be run or climbed by me that day?

Do I ultra-run because my body loves to be what it evolved to be, and at an unconscious level is it urging me to be more authentically me? Is this why I run ultras?

My hunch, in my sedentary first-world life of comfort, food I don't have to hunt or scavenge for, and leisure opportunities, is that when I run into the forest my unconscious archaic mind finds much joy in activities and hardships that feel intuitively right. Is it delighted when I move, chase, flee, and endure?

Perhaps joy is a part of my *why*.

Perhaps joy is the reward.

And not surprisingly, can it also be said that when I relent to the pull to do these things, I rediscover my original *self* in some esoteric way?

If that's true, then have I just taken the long trail to get to Mallory and Messner's finish lines ... the ones Roberts, and I, originally debunked ... and isn't getting there the long hard way what ultrarunners always do? And was Roberts onto something, too? Not necessarily that we are all wired for risk, but maybe something simpler: that we humans are genetically predisposed to thrive through rigorous motion in conjunction with one another—the exact experience that surviving his adventures delivered to him.

Why did I decide to challenge myself to endure 100 continuous miles on my own two feet before I turned sixty? Why do I run ultras? Because what I am at my evolutionary core urges me to move, and flee, and chase in tandem with others of my running community in the wilds of nature, and when I experience these things in my modern life, I find joy ... and I find myself.

Far from Old

The last leg of the ultra is when you discover
what you are
and it's the trail along which
a reconnection to your ancient self
might just be made.

CHAPTER 14

Revenge Run

Scattered clouds above the Tantalus Range are whitening with increasing brightness along their wispy eastern edges, while Junction Park in downtown Squamish lingers in the shadow of the Stawamus Chief towering across the inlet, its murky face fracture-lined, yet beckoning. Dawn has brightened the sky just enough to light my way. I take off my headlamp and tuck it into a side pouch on my hydration pack, thankful that it's not dark and rainy.

It's 5:20 a.m., August 20, 2022, and once again, I'm in the starting corral of a Squamish50-Mile race, four months after my 100-miler.

Am I ready?

Over the past weeks, I believed I was, but with the glossy black start/finish arch ahead of me, doubt seeps in. The last time I passed through this gateway, in that unforgiving October deluge ten months ago, I didn't return. My hands touch the scars on my cold thighs. The memories of my chafing DNF give me goosebumps. My stomach goes hollow when I remind myself that not only must I make it to the end today, I must also make it to the end again tomorrow to attain my 50/50 finisher cap.

I'm sixty years old, and I highly doubt that a chance to complete this challenge will come around another time for me. After eighteen months of continuous training for a 50/50 DNF, my HomeRun100, and this 50/50, I know I've reached my physical limit. I will need to rest. Our five granddaughters are getting to ages where they feel like little people to me. I'm a people person, not a baby person. What spending choices will I make in the coming decade with the limited currency of time allotted to me?

The chance to stand in this starting corral, for potentially the last time, to avenge last October's defeat, is what I've been craving in recent days. But now, for the first time, the memory of the way I failed has me truly scared. I wasn't scared yesterday, or the day before. This fear is new and concerning. It's not my historic starting line fear of being inadequate to the task. It's a visceral fear of physical calamity that's shaking my confidence like no race start before.

I finished 100 miles. I will repeat this mantra often and hold it up as a sword in the face of my fear. *I can do this.*

Bushy-red-bearded Gary Robbins, race director, capped in a bright red running hat, is up to his usual antics with the pre-race briefing. His headlamp illuminates his note sheets, and they radiate like a sideways barcode. They also reflect a stark white light back onto his face. He is a glowing not-one-ounce-of-fat garden gnome standing on a podium barking instructions at us. He gets the international racers to cheer for themselves when he announces their countries. He waves his cigarette-pack-sized pink flags on their stiff thin wires, promising us that we will see at least one every minute of the day to guide our way. He gets everyone to boisterously shout, "Wrong way!" when he holds up the white sign with the bold black "X." I watch the first-time runners react to him. He's winning them over like he always does. He reminisces a bit about the hideous conditions of last year's race. *Come on, man, don't go there. I'm trying to forget that.* But I laugh along with everyone else.

Then it's "Three. Two. One. GO!" and an emotional start to the race for me.

Passing under the arch, I intimately know what lies ahead and how much I will suffer. The fear that's clutching me leans in close and whispers it will gut me with a DNF. My fight reflexes trigger at the thought of being bloodied again by this enemy. I run the first hundred metres along Cleveland Avenue and promise myself I will rage and claw my way to the end.

———

I run with the pack for the first 5 kilometres before implementing my *four-and-one* pacing strategy. The first 5 kilometres are all adrenaline and eagerness and tight sections of single track and too many runners. It isn't until I get on the dike adjacent to the Mamquam River that I can drop to the side and speed-hike my minutes. Runners pass and immediately ask if I'm OK. "Yes," I assure them, and watch them run ahead, confused as to why I stopped running with 75 kilometres still to go. I will inevitably overtake a few of them by the first aid station.

A chorus of Capra volunteers shout "Randy!" as I approach, and we high-five as I move through the aid station quickly, not needing to stop for fuel or water. Solana definitely broke open her tickle-trunk of onesies this morning. Eleven multi-coloured Capra animals crew the station. Three pink rabbits. The Grinch. A piñata. Rainbow beasts and possibly a walrus. A blue and white dinosaur storms around among them. Annie is a dragon holding a rotund vampire bat. "Annie you're weird!" I call out. A great celebration of 10 kilometres done. These are my people, and I love them. I run off smiling, six minutes ahead of my race plan. The fear is waning.

Four kilometres later I cross Hop Ranch Creek, and waiting on the other side, at the trailhead of Crouching Squirrel Hidden Monkey, are Cindy and several of our neighbours; Merdad, Katie, and Steph, along with Kelly and Karina from my HomeRun100. More cheering and clapping. Much gratitude.

Up DeBeck's I go. No waterfall climbs to slosh through this time on Rigs In Zen, just dry August dirt, the kind that can make the rock as slippery as ice. Nature is rarely idyllic; mostly, it is mildly malevolent. I make the top in good shape and down DeBeck's I run, feeling strong. After a few kilometres of glorious forest, Suzanne hands me my next batch of fuel and tops up my water at the Alice Lake aid station. I immediately depart, four minutes ahead of race plan.

———

My journey to the Corners aid station is methodical, as is my loop around the Garibaldi Highlands on rising and falling thickly wooded trails with names—Of Mice and Men and Entrails—as engrossing as their beauty. I'm executing as trained and as per plan. I conclude my loop back at Corners, one minute behind race plan, six hours into the race.

The fear I felt in the starting corral returns as I depart Corners and run/hike the forest service road to the Galactic Scheisse climb trail. I have no reason to be worried from a physical standpoint: I'm fit, the day is warm, maybe it's getting a bit too muggy, although the humidity is of little concern in the coolness of the trees. But Galactic is stressful from a mental perspective.

On the trail, I experience palpable dread as I climb through sections where the freezing water numbed my feet and chilled me to the core ten months earlier. My breathing has an anxious quickness to it as I approach the gully where I found the hypothermic runner who had slipped and submerged in an icy torrent. Today there isn't even a trickle of water. Galactic is one big bad memory. It feels as endless as it did when my gear started to chew me to pieces. The energy exerted on every leg lift is compounded near the top by a desire to just get this done and get out of here. A small band of runners chugs past me, chattering a mile a minute, making me feel slow. Anxious breaths increase.

Then I crest the summit, drop to the wooden bridge, rise up

again, and finally start the long winding descent to the Word of Mouth aid station. I arrive twenty-one minutes behind target. My fear opened the door for mental exertion to take its toll earlier than usual, and uncertainty made the climb more difficult than it should have been. Displeased with being behind at the midway point, I find some relief in having put Galactic behind me and I focus on picking up a bit of speed through the newly rerouted and loamy Word of Mouth trail. The spongy nature of the fresh trail presents unexpected challenges and I lose my balance and fall a few times. My arms prickle with hundreds of tiny bark mulch splinters that bristle in barbed anger when I rub my hand over the skin they now infest.

———

Solana, Suzanne, Liberty, and Amish greet me with cheers 100 metres out from the creek where Annie took my *drenched and done* photo last year. The creek bed is dry when we cross it today.

I climb the concrete stairs to the central courtyard of Quest University with my friends at my side and spectators clapping and shouting encouragement from where they sit in little knots strewn across the grassy slope. This is the site of my bloody horrible DNF in the October 2021 atmospheric river. Today is different. My two-day revenge run is underway, and comparatively, things are under control. I'm only fifteen minutes off my target and moving well, 53 kilometres into day one's 80 kilometres. No chafing.

I spot Cindy and Jacquelyn in the crew area with supply pack and cooler at the ready. Karina from my HomeRun100 is there, and Annie, too. My running clan, five of whom will be racing tomorrow. There's a strong feeling that we're all in this together.

I toss my hydration pack to Cindy, knowing she will carry out her part of the plan and restock it with water, gels, and Tailwind for the next leg of my race. In return, she tosses me a Ziploc bag with a container of lube and some sanitary wipes.

"Thanks!" I give her a thumbs up and head for the nearest blue-plastic portable potty. I toss a look back at the crew as I grab the door handle and see that Jacquelyn is already helping Cindy empty my sweat-soaked pack. Both have their determined nursing faces on—functioning with objective precision. The chop-chop, get-it-done tone of their voices would have told me the same without the glance.

It's great to see everyone here on a day when I'm still very much in the game. I'm not letting the crew down on this 50/50. That alone feels so good.

"Five minutes!" Suzanne shouts at me as I close the potty door.

"Have mercy, woman," I want to say in return, but I smirk instead. She's on her game and enjoying every bit of ordering me around—with the goal of getting me to the finish line. Meeting the crew is not about fun and games this weekend. It's about executing a carefully thought-out plan to get to the finish line.

"Four minutes!" reverberates through the blue biffy.

Is she standing right outside?

"Yeah. Yeah. I'm getting things done!" I shout back. My voice booms in the mildly rancid cubicle. I get what she's doing. Planning for this weekend we studied my HomeRun100 crew sheet and saw how much time I wasted in aid stations. It's abundantly clear that Suzanne is not going to let that happen today!

Out of the john and back over to the crew; Cindy quizzes me about how my calorie intake is going. I tell her my stomach is turning a bit. We both agree that the humidity has become oppressive and will get worse as we move toward peak heat around 6 p.m.

"Three minutes," Suzanne says, then quickly adds, "Cindy, did you check his garbage?"

"He says he threw his wrappers out at Word of Mouth."

"Did you?" Suzanne glares at me.

"Yes."

"Don't lie."

"Yes! I ate everything on my list, and I had chips and pop and some candy at Word of Mouth. I'm good."

"How much water did he need? Is he drinking? Did he finish his Tailwind?"

Hey, you can ask me, I'm right here.

"Tailwind was all gone. He's not drinking enough water, though."

Tattled on by my wife!

Cindy drapes the ice collar she made for my Javelina Jundred around my neck. With stern, clinical efficiency she clips the ends of the ice sausage together at my chest and smooths out the lumps at the back of my neck. She doesn't make eye contact.

Does she look concerned because she's trying to get me out of here fast or is she sending a message about my hydration? I take a deep breath and help her make the adjustments.

Damn this thing is cold! But I know I need it. The heat and humidity are taking their toll and will get worse on Climb Trail coming up. And she's right, I wasn't drinking enough on my descent from the top of Galactic because my gut was turning. I will do my best to fix that. I promise my crew that I will focus on hydration.

"Time's up! Does he have everything?"

Cindy and Suzanne double-check my pack pouches and are happy with what they see. I trust that my pack's new contents match what I put on the plan—no need to fiddle with any details for the moment. We're on target.

As I depart the Quest aid station and set out on the final third of my Saturday 50-miler, I think to myself that apart from some tummy upset, this is going to be an uneventful, perhaps boring race from here on out. I'm past last year's disaster point, and though things today are running a wee bit slow, I'm close enough to plan that I'm not overly concerned. My legs feel ready for the next climb.

———

Excessive humidity, uncommon to the West Coast, overtakes me that afternoon. Seven-to-eight kilometres out from Quest, my stomach takes a dramatic downturn and my strength dwindles. By Garibaldi aid station, I am thirty-five minutes off my target time and flirting with disaster. I do not move with purpose through the non-stop climbs and descents of the next twisting section of the course. At Far Side aid station, I make it out a mere seven minutes before the 7:30 p.m. cutoff.

How can this be happening with a 50K race still to be completed tomorrow? Where did the solid base of a spring 100-miler and months of climb training through the summer go?

It's as though I ran away from the Quest aid station and into an entirely different race, run by an entirely different me.

After Cindy and Jacquelyn take care of my pack supplies at Far Side and express their growing fear about how dehydrated I'm getting, Solana walks with me out onto the final leg. Her pep talk is a good one (I wish I could remember it now!), and she makes sure I eat half a Long John—the only food I'm not gagging on. Her Aussie Shepard, Zeus, my orange-brown, cream and grey trail friend, tags along and his derp face and leg licks lift my spirits.

After a few hundred metres, Solana calls Zeus to her side and she sends me on my way. Her long day of tirelessly working her store and supporting her running friends on the racecourse finally ends, and, like Jacquelyn, she will head off to bed to rest up for her own Sunday race, along with Suzanne, Karina, and Amish, whom I assume are already doing the same. I continue to slug it out in the darkness. I have 10 kilometres to go.

The day-one 50-miler tears me up. Grossly dehydrated from the energy-sapping heat and humidity through the late afternoon (even though I managed my liquids well), under-fuelled due to excessive nausea, and demoralized by my lack of strength on the final climbs, I travel the final kilometres through the forests of Smoke Bluffs alone in my headlamp's bubble of light. Nothing is as I want it to be.

Five years earlier I moved joyfully through this final stretch, encouraging a co-runner to move a bit faster with me. Now, the day's weather and eighteen months of continual training and racing—the last ten done in preparation for this revenge run—are piling on as unrelenting fatigue.

I am pushing my physical and mental capabilities far past their boundaries, all the while becoming ever more unsteady. I slide into a mental cavern as dark as the forest around me. At the bottom of it, despondency seeks to embrace me in its bony arms, to amplify my exhaustion, to wither my hope, to steal my courage. My eyes bulge as I struggle to keep the darkness inside my forehead from closing in and trapping me with its demon. Three-and-a-half kilometres to go.

"Randy?"

I see a headlamp flickering through the trees up ahead. "Yeah?" I recognize the voice, but my mind, straining against the ensnaring darkness, doesn't click on who it is. *No one cheers runners out here—especially this late.*

"Buddy! I've been waiting for you! Oh my God, the bats are crazy. I almost left, but Solana kept texting that she could see you getting closer to me on her app."

Amish. Here in the dark. Waiting to cheer me on. In the pit of my despair. I am dumbfounded by gratitude.

"How are you, man?" Amish's voice is full of concern, the same concern I heard in Solana's voice as she walked me out of the last aid station and sent me off into the dark. It's obvious that my friends want me to bag this 50/50 as much as I do, and even more obvious that I'm not proving to them that I can do it.

Amish walks alongside me to the nearby parking lot. I tell him the day has been tougher than I expected. I tell him I don't have a clue how I'm going to get up tomorrow morning and make it to the start line of the 50K. I share with him how tragic that will be because this is probably the last shot I have in my life to get the 50/50. The finality of watching this opportunity slip away has been adding weight to each of my footsteps over the past kilometres.

Amish offers a welcome listening ear and much encouragement. His belief in me is tangible.

I part with Amish at the deserted Smoke Bluffs parking lot. His sudden appearance has done wonders, pulling my mind partway out of the cavern and away from despondency, setting me on a more positive path to the finish line.

I am forever grateful for Amish's solitary headlamp in the dark, and for Solana, who, while lying in bed watching a GPS signal when she should have been sleeping in anticipation of *her* race, pushed a team Capra member beyond the call of duty to support a fellow runner late in the evening, the night before *his* own race. Their encouragement, their sacrifices, exemplify the spirit of the trail community I have the good fortune to run with.

In the end, I cross the finish line at 9:40 p.m. Running time 16:10:03. Forty minutes off my target time. Fifty minutes ahead of race cutoff. Fifth out of the six guys in the M60-69 bracket to get back to the start/finish arch. Runner 219 out of 231 to make it home.

Two strides past the timing strip, Race Director Gary Robbins captures me in his patented *You did it!* hug. I don't fully embrace him in return. I haven't done it—yet. I still have one more race to complete.

"It was hard today, Gary," is all I can mutter.

"It's supposed to be hard," he replies as he holds my shoulders and gives me a tight-lipped smile with one eyebrow cocked—the right message for the moment. In his face, I can see he wants me to finish this hard thing that he personally challenged me to accomplish a few years earlier. That's what inspired me in the first place.

Back in 2019, before the pandemic delays and my 2021 abraded DNF, Gary believed I could do it.

Cindy and Amish wait nearby. My plan for this finish line moment was to be as pumped and excited as I had been when I finished my previous SQ50-Miler five years earlier—the night I knew I could go another 20 kilometres and pull off 100K. Instead, I am destroyed like no race has wrecked me for many years.

I am embarrassed and angered. I repeat two sentences as we move through the finish line winddown and head to the Jeep. "I don't know how I'm going to start tomorrow," and "I can't finish what I don't start." I am totally conflicted, and with everything so mixed up in my head, and apparently my stomach too, I puke my post-race burger on the drive home.

———

A shower. Chicken soup. Cindy's focus on getting me re-hydrated. A last-minute gift of a borrowed set of compression pants. All these positive interventions physically realign me. I'm down six pounds on the day and apprehensive, no, terrified of how I will feel when I'm supposed to get back on my feet in a few hours. *Will I even be able to walk?*

I can't finish what I don't start.

I cling to those seven words as the mantra that will get me to my 4:30 a.m. wake up and then across the 6:15 a.m. Squamish50K start line. I choose to let go of *I don't know how*, and force it from my mind.

On the couch, compression pants kneading my legs like so much sore dough, slurping soup, I make up my mind that I will haul myself out of bed at 4:30 a.m. no matter how awful I feel—*I will cross the start line of the SQ50K*. If I walk 200 metres out, turn around, and hand in my bib, I will have done more than many others—I will have started day two. I am not going to let day one of the 50/50 defeat me again. To start day two will be more than I accomplished the year before.

At midnight I fall asleep with one goal: to walk across the SQ50K starting line in six hours.

———

Making the decision to fight my way across that Sunday start line and attempt to complete the 50/50 at age sixty was about achieving a life goal, and more viscerally, avenging the loss of that goal ten months before. An ambition powered by the fear that I might not have it in me to get to that level of fitness in my life ever again. In terms of a 50/50 finish, there was a lot on the line. But, beyond capturing a finisher cap, there was another, deeper motivation that underpinned my desire to overcome the physical exhaustion and pain and my desire to take the easy road and just call it quits that night—a motivation I never anticipated.

At the start of my training block four months earlier, my eighty-eight-year-old dad was diagnosed with a sudden and aggressive cancer. Two questions needed answering right up front: at what stage was the cancer, and would Dad opt for treatment if treatment was even an option? It took a month to determine those two answers—a distressing life-on-hold period for everyone.

Early in the seemingly endless investigation process, the option to give in to the cancer and not cross the treatment starting line was a tantalizing and almost favourable one. Given the aggressive nature of the cancer he was stricken with, Dad stacked the thin likelihood of late-stage treatment success against the unavoidable hardships that would batter both him and Mom during the months-long battle he would wage. If the cancer had progressed quite far, letting it take its course had its merits as an end-of-life choice.

Then came the reprieve. Dad's cancer, though fast-growing and menacing to see, was still at stage one in terms of its full-body impact. In an in-depth question-filled session, his oncologist presented us with a robust chemo and radiation plan to wipe the disease out before it became irreversible. Stunned by the revelation of a greater-than-expected chance for success, Dad and Mom reoriented and chose the hard road of treatment—a fight they would power with faith.

It was impossible to balance work, family, training for an ultra, and assisting with a cancer battle. In the end, I did most chores as best I could and nothing well. Being faced with a loved one's mortality also clarified my goals and priorities. When Dad was first diagnosed it looked like the summer of 2022 would be the second summer in a row that cancer took a parent from Cindy and me. Cindy's mom's care and passing required Cindy to take a leave of absence from the ER. I looked ahead and expected my role and commitments would be much the same.

During the early June cancer appointment parade, my training was put on hold and my 50/50 almost abandoned. Then, when Dad chose to endure, my return to training became my way of grinding through his treatment with him. Though I shared little of my running exploits with Mom and Dad through July and August—they were overwhelmed as it was—pushing through exhaustion on long runs felt like bonding when I would later spend time with Dad and he would nod off, haggard and listless, two characteristics that had never defined him.

Through that summer, our existences could not have been more dichotomous. I, the bald one, got stronger and stronger. Dad, the gentleman who sported that lush silvery flat-top that all the ladies in their seniors' tower loved, weakened more every day. Out on their balcony on a warm August night, I shaved the final whisps of his hair away.

Dad, the speed walking, volunteer coffee-serving, wise-cracking old guy who never looked nearly as old as he was, suffered as the chemo treatments took him close to death in the great hope

that the cancer would die before he did. As he concluded chemo-
therapy, the week of the 50/50, he was heading toward the lowest
of his lows.

With all my dad was going through, and given how hard he
was fighting, how could I not choose to get my ass out of bed to
attempt something I was trained for and ready to do? That I might
never get the chance to accomplish my 50/50 goal again was made
poignantly clear through the lens of my dad's circumstances. Dad
was not quitting. I would honour that. I would not accept the loss
of my life goal without at least crossing the start line.

———

The 4:30 a.m. alarm rouses me from a restful sleep. To my utter
amazement, *I'm ready*.

A quick shower and a bowl of Cheerios wake me fully. I'm
stiff and sore but moving and pulling on my running gear without
problems. I look in the mirror and see myself in my Capra tank top.
I had put this top aside specifically for today—I want to cross the
finish line with my team logo right out front. The Capra community helped get me to this point. I have many reasons to get across
the start line today—this top bears witness to yet another.

Cindy pilots Jaquelyn and me the short drive to the drop-off
point on the highway at the entry to Alice Lake. Few words are
exchanged. I find myself perplexed by the surreal nature of what's
transpiring. The trip is a befuddled blur. Four and a half hours
of sleep and somehow I'm getting out of the Jeep on a roadside
bustling with ultrarunners, and my route home is 50 kilometres
long. Even more unfathomable, after last night's dehydrated stag-
ger across the timing mats, I can walk.

Cindy wishes us luck through the open passenger side window, spins her head to shoulder-check the bumper-car traffic of all
the runner deliveries, picks her opening, and escapes. Watching

her dart away, I once again conclude that she should have raced cars. If a miracle happens, the next time she sees me will be at the Quest aid station, halfway into the race.

I test my legs on the 500-metre walk to the starting corral. Jacquelyn quizzes me on how I feel the whole way. There is pain but no injury. Range of motion is good enough to start and should get better as I warm up. I tell her I'm going to trust that all those back-to-back long training days will pay off today. Somehow, the finish on day two of those is always better than day one. It's uncanny how that works.

After last night's debacle of a 50-mile finish, I find it hard to believe that I'm actually nearing the 50K starting area until I hear ever-jovial and bespectacled Race Announcer John Crosby making wisecracks about runners close to his booth. *This is real.*

I flinch at the ceaseless door slams whamming along the line of portable biffies like an ill-timed rifle salute. Each sharp *Crack!* jars me more fully awake. I take it all in, the festive bustle of the pre-race, and it all feels like a fluke, even though I have trained for months—years—to be in this place. But will I ever shake my imposter syndrome?

In the corral, Jacquelyn takes a selfie with me and my HomeRun100 midnight pacing duo, Kelly and Karina. We're a mixed bag of agendas. Kelly is outright gunning for the female 50K win today. After long pandemic layoffs from racing, Jacquelyn and Karina are fighting their own demons of doubt. Both are all nerves, neither convinced that they won't DNF.

I am here for race number two of my 50/50. This is my now-or-never moment. It is good medicine to be in the crowded corral with these three and several other running acquaintances from Capra and elsewhere. We are all here, snug, touching each other as we shift nervously on our feet; a rippling conglomeration of humans designed to run long distances and endure great pain. We are about to move and chase and suffer in concert over 50 kilometres of mountain single track. At the finish line, those who survive it will celebrate their safe return home with those awaiting them. Many new bonds that begin to form in the corral will cement by day's end as runners, previously unknown to each other, unite in the re-creation of the struggle as old as our species.

In an odd juxtaposition to this bonding, during the Gary Robbins pre-race briefing, Jacquelyn, Karina, Kelly, and I all wish each other the best and separate to get into our own headspaces and prepare to run our own races. Together, as individuals, is how we will take on the challenges of the day.

The timing clock winds down, and John Crosby gets the runners to shout out, "Three. Two. One. GO!"

Well back in the corral, I see the heads of the elite runners beneath the starting arch rise and break forward. Seconds later, the entire corral of bobbing heads is in motion, and I, grateful that I did not quit when it all felt hopeless mere hours ago, am caught up in the flow of ultrarunners funnelling toward the arch.

I don't walk across the start line as I promised myself I would. I run.

———

Slower than I'd like to be on the rolling trail beside Stump Lake, while at the same time stunned that I am actually *in this race*, I suck up the foot and calf pain I'm so familiar with. The bulging agony of unyielding muscles persists along the Bob McIntosh Memorial Trail and takes my breath from me on the long flat section through the forest where I really want to run and make good time. The Dead End Loop instigates a mental scrap between what I want to do and what I can do. I work hard at relaxing when the pain is too great to run. I'm hiking with purpose. *Go with this. Don't give up.* I'm waiting for myself to suddenly fall completely apart … but, somehow, I keep hoisting myself up the inclines and shuffling the declines. The nearby rapids-rush of the Cheekye River signals a warning that the day's first significant climb awaits ahead.

Screaming tight at the start of the steep Made in the Shade switchbacks, my knotted calves finally release on one of the final hairpins and I'm able to run again after I ascend the remainder of the hill. My strides are smooth along the zigzag descent of Rob's Corners. I feel joy for the first time in the weekend. I didn't feel joy on the 50-mile yesterday—its absence contributing to how disheartened I became.

Eight kilometres in, at bustling Corners aid station, I'm only four minutes over target time. *Unbelievable*. Getting here in good time after such a painful start has me smiling and cheerily greeting all the volunteers. I loosen up even more on the forest service road approach to Galactic. I feel stronger now than in the starting corral.

I hike Galactic's lush green fern-lined ascending causeway consistently from bottom to top, passing other runners along the way. *Oh, the joy of running a 50K with lots of newbies to slowly pick off once they tucker out after their over-zealous start.* I work hard to not let my face show how victorious I feel each time I overtake someone.

"Slow and steady!" I cheer. "Keep up that pace!" I clap and encourage and climb away from them, almost giddy because today I'm beating the mountain that beat me so badly. My body feels stronger today than it did yesterday.

I don't fall in the needle-like mulch on Word of Mouth and end up enjoying some trail time with a Capra runner as we both hurry along. Emerging from the trail onto the university grounds, I'm greeted by Sunday's cheering crowd on the grassy bank that drops off the Quest courtyard. As I climb the stairs and chat with a few folks I know, I see Cindy at the ready, and with her, Jen and Jennie. I'm delighted that they've driven up from Vancouver to encourage their large contingent of friends in today's races. Their presence makes the day even more joyful. No Suzanne, or Solana, or Amish today. They have long since finished off their SQ23Ks and are no doubt enjoying the party at Junction Park.

Once again, Cindy makes sure my pack is prepped with fuel, Tailwind, and water, and she laces the ice collar around my neck. The temperature is rising, and though less humid than yesterday, she and I both know how stifling the STP Trail is going to get. Anything I can do to keep my core cool in that tepid valley this afternoon will be a benefit.

Jennie has multi-coloured Freezies. I double-fist a blue and yellow, and joke, "Blue, stay in the Matrix. Yellow, embrace the crappy reality of this race." I enjoy my own humour like I enjoy both Freezies.

It's exciting to hear about Kelly's race to this point—that she was fighting for the lead when she passed through Quest. Cindy also reports that she crewed both Karina and Jacquelyn and that both were in good shape and in great spirits.

So many from the Capra gang are chasing the finish, and five hours in and one big mountain down, I'm only twelve minutes behind target.

———

I approach Climb Trail knowing it's been my nemesis in the past. Even though Galactic is the longest climb of the Squamish50 races, Climb Trail's 450 vertical metres of continuous elevation gain with countless false summits on repetitive switchbacks gave me problems in each of my three previous races. Yesterday, when I came upon it two-thirds deep in the 50-mile, it sucked the life out of me again. I just don't enjoy this hill—except for today.

Back in the starting corral, I told Jacquelyn and Karina how much I was dreading this section of the course, and Jacquelyn reminded me that her dad, my best buddy Glenn, would approach it *one step at a time*. She was right, of course.

At the trailhead, I dedicate the climb to Glenn and start grinding up, one step at a time. Every upward stride hurts everywhere. It's not one pain here and another there at this stage. It's ache. All over. Glenn would understand. That's what makes the hard steps meaningful to me. I choose to experience the climb in the context of shared suffering with a friend rather than have a meaningless and negative climbing experience. It's a way of getting through the upward grind.

It's also getting hotter, and my ice collar is melting faster than I'd like. I open one end and start chewing on the ice to gain some instant relief when the sun cooks me on a section of exposed trail. The crunch of the ice between my teeth is so loud in my head that I don't realize another runner is overtaking me. I'm startled when a tiny lady catches up to me and strikes up a conversation.

It's Vicki Romanin, and she will finish as the oldest 50/50 female this year. I'm inspired by a story she tells me about a 200-kilometre stage race she did in the Alps. Vicki does for me on this trail what Ann, the revenge runner, did for me in 2017 on the DeBeck's climb: she takes my mind off the task at hand with a story. Or should I say stories. I can only dream of doing what Vicki's done in her ultrarunning life. Her company along these few kilometres of trail is a gift. We summit Climb Trail, run down the curving water-slide-like Angry M with its steep-banked mountain bike corners, and once we hit the forest service road, we run farther down to the Garibaldi aid station, arriving five minutes over my target time. Somehow, I lose Vicki at this point, but the lift I received from her is already more than enough.

I eat a bunch of pickles at Garibaldi and a fist full of ripple chips. Nothing else is appealing apart from salt and pickle juice, a clear dehydration warning sign. I fill both of my Tailwind soft flasks to provide 400 calories over the next two hours. A cheery aid station volunteer tops up my hydration pack's water reservoir, and away I go with 18 kilometres of my 130-kilometre weekend yet to be covered.

———

As expected, the push through the STP valley is a hot one, and for the first time today, my engine starts to sputter. This had to happen eventually. I'm amazed it took this long to start conking out. I thought I would falter on Climb Trail, but Vicki's appearance staved that off.

Climbing up out of the valley to Bonsai Trail, my stomach turns, and the solid foods and gels I try to put in come back out of my mouth with loud gagging sounds. They don't even make it to the back of my throat. It's going to be Tailwind to the end with maybe some sugary snacks at Far Side. I'm less than four hours from the finish line, and the absence of solid or gel calories over that timeframe does not meet my quit criteria. Deciding, up on Bonsai, that I'm good with Tailwind to the end is a relief. I will not worry about calories anymore this weekend. I am freed as I start to descend the Somewhere Over There Trail that will lead to the bridge overlooking the Mamquam Falls.

Entering Far Side aid station, I pass through a towering re-creation of the Jurassic Park front gate, complete with fake torches spouting red and yellow tissue paper flames up both sides and a bold, red-lettered, "Jurassic Far Side" sign scratched across the top. I navigate past a volunteer riding an inflatable T-Rex and two others whose bellies are ringed by dino pool floaties to find Cindy by the tents. I tell her I'm OK with nothing but emergency gel calories in my pack. I will consume Tailwind calories only now. She's good with my decision to go liquids to the end. She makes sure my Tailwind and water are topped up for the final 10 kilometres, and as quick as that, I'm ready to depart.

But no sooner do I say, "Liquids only," than I see watermelon in a big bowl on the food tent table and grab a piece in each hand. I eat watermelon. Quite a bit of watermelon. My body is so fickle when I'm this cooked. I can't even begin guessing what it wants from one minute to the next.

Then I leave Jurassic Far Side for the second and last time this weekend. The dinosaur eggs littering the trail on the way out, some hatching dino stuffies, have me smiling more today than they did yesterday. Today is, without a doubt, more joyful.

———

The approach trails to the final Mountain of Phlegm climb are a labyrinth of thickly wooded twists and crossovers and inevitable wrong turns when unflagged. Even when flagged, the approach can give a fresh runner a sense of being lost. Slowly succumbing to exhaustion, I feel doubly lost.

Did the flaggers get this turn right? This doesn't feel right. I think I should be going up there, not around that. Did something change here since I came through last night? It felt quicker last night—even though I was slow. I should see that curved tree with the boulder by it soon. Why am I not seeing it yet? This intertwined section of densely forested hillside is making me anxious.

But not as anxious as the runner who comes up behind me on a hopscotch downhill littered with slick stones and tight undergrowth.

"There's not enough time to finish this," she says and squeezes by. Her voice is high and tense.

"Well, you caught up with me, and I'm going to finish," I reply with a smile she doesn't see. Then I offer some calm reassurance: "You're definitely going to finish this race."

She disappears ahead of me around a tight turn. I don't think she even heard me.

I catch her on the next short climb, where the uphill is challenging her. It's my turn to squeeze past.

"I'm too slow going up!" The panic in her voice makes her words bite as if she's berating me.

"But you're moving really well apart from that. Just one step at a time going up. The last 5 kilometres to the finish are all downhill and flat. You've got this."

"How many more uphills?

"Two little ones, maybe three, then the last climb to the towers. That's it. You can do this."

We leapfrog each other over the next few sets of climbs before she once again bursts past me on a longer section of runnable trail.

"I'm not going to finish!"

"Yes, you are!" I call after her. *Are we going to fight about this?*

I pass her again on the next gradual uphill and when I arrive at the last steep finale, I throw a glance back down the slope and don't see her behind me anymore. I know she will finish; she's moving well enough for that. I just wish she wasn't being swept to the end by panic. What I really want to do is drop back and give her a pep talk about how finishing is in her mind, not her legs, and convince her that her mind isn't in the right place, and then help her change that, but this is not the time for that little lecture. She will finish, and it will be stressful.

———

On the top of the Mountain of Phlegm Trail, I know how far I still have to go, I know the terrain, I know what I've got left in the tank, and I know I will finish before cutoff.

The question is: *Will I finish well?*

I climb up onto the wooden Mountain FM radio tower platform, look at my watch, grapple with some simple math, and conclude that if I run from here, I can make my target of finishing race number two in under eleven hours.

To the north, I see DeBeck's, the narrow mountain I looped last April with Jacquelyn and Jen on my HomeRun100. To the south stands the Stawamus Chief that hovered over me, monolithic and brooding, while I toiled beneath it with Suzanne and Sachi in the darkest hours of that same event. How I will finish becomes clear in these memories.

I will avenge my one regret from that 100-miler.

Jen, Jacquelyn, and Jennie put a challenge before me that beautiful April morning: run to the finish and achieve my "A" goal. In response, I chose to ease my way to the finish and get my "B" goal. Ever since, I have felt like I didn't honour them with my decision. They believed in me. I should have accepted their challenge. I had nothing to lose by leaving it all out there and failing. My "B" goal would still have been attained, and by giving my "A" goal a legitimate shot, I would have done away with any lingering remorse for not trying. I stepped away from a no-lose proposition on the way to that finish line. I regret that.

Today will be different.

I hop off the platform and crash in slow, muscle-straining motion awkwardly to the ground. My feet and knees and back cry out. *That wasn't smart. Why would I do that after beating myself up for 125 kilometres?* I laugh out loud. I imagine my joints creaking as I get up. Perhaps they do.

I'm acutely aware of how stiff and sore my legs are. I hobble down the trail with a loping, tentative gait. Where I should run, I shuffle briskly. The descent of the sheer, long-drop Smoke Bluffs staircases offers a combination of jolting pain and head-spinning dizziness. I hold onto the rails for dear life. The best I can do along the bike path through Rose Park is a run/walk. At the "1 KM" remaining sign, just beyond the bridge underpass, I look at my watch. I have a little less than ten minutes to make my "A" goal.

To run is hellish. Each leg lift seizes to a halt before it's fulfilled. My feet jerkily swing forward to hard landings. I'm an inflexible robot with too little oil. I turn at last onto Loggers Lane, new condos on my left, a commercial back alley with garbage bins to dodge when cars approach on my right. Bystanders are sprinkled here and there, cheering. Emotion overtakes me. I hope I don't ugly cry too much when I get to the finish line gauntlet at Junction Park.

The visceral fear of seconds ticking closer to eleven hours ratchets up. My senses elevate, and I'm on the razor's edge between crystal clarity and complete confusion.

Am I chasing the finish or fleeing failure?

It's that rare, exhausted, dissociative moment when the run itself is outside of time. It's a rush that almost stands still.

I feel so alive. Chasing an arbitrary cutoff time inside my head means nothing … and yet it means everything because of what I'm experiencing to beat it.

Solana is on the road by the gate to the park. She unleashes my trail buddy, Zeus, to run to the finish line with me. Zeus leads the way through the waist-high rail gate held open by a spectator and bounds ahead. The music is blaring at the unseen party half the park away. We enter the tree-lined funnel to the finish line. Along the temporary fences beneath the pines, cedars, maples, spruce, and cherries I see the exuberant faces of the Capra clan and hear their shouts and laughter—the fraternity of runners whose friendships are forged in footsteps. Cindy stands beneath the arch. Behind her are Krystina and granddaughters Lizzy and Kat. John Crosby calls out, "Rrrrandy Klassen! 50/50!" over the loudspeakers. I'm home.

I cross the timing mat in 10:57:17.

It's over in an instant. The transcendence of those last 5 kilometres, as I pushed myself way past my boundaries and felt what it was *to be that*, doesn't mean anything to anyone but me. My finish line joy is akin to a sudden and unexpected upwelling of grief—only it's not grief's unanticipated sorrow that wracks my body, it is an inexplicable wave of exhilaration that comes from surviving the quest and at last being *safe*.

Gary Robbins grins and presses a blue and tan baseball cap firmly onto my sweaty head. Silver lettering reads: "Squamish50/50 Finisher." Best prize ever.

———

I crossed the line as the oldest male finisher of the 50/50 in 2022. M60-69 1/1. There was something deeply satisfying in that stat, and in knowing I chose to finish well, with no regrets.

And my three clanswomen from the starting corral? After duelling for the lead for the first half of the race, Kelly suffered serious leg cramps and finished sixth female overall. And to no one's surprise, apart from maybe their own, strong runners Jacquelyn and Karina both finished with good times on a hot and difficult day of racing. Suzanne, Solana, Sachi, and Amish all sported Squamish23K medals in our group photo. Many more from the Capra community crossed their 23K and 50K finish lines that day as well.

Cindy and I and the Capra gang celebrated for a long time at Junction Park. We cheered wildly for the last runners, all of whom responded to the crowd's cries of encouragement and pushed beyond themselves to run their last few metres before crashing, utterly spent, into Gary's arms beneath the black finisher's arch. More tears were shed. It felt good to cry for joy.

Finally, the sweepers arrived. It was done.

Those who could make it home, did—fulfilling an ancient wisdom that connects us to our distant past and our design, harkening to an instinctive awareness tied to what we are, heeding the pull that gets us out to do that hard thing all over again to see if we can survive.

Afterword

My hope is that when runners of all persuasions read this book, it reminds them of their own stories. I hope they cherish those stories, the people they ran with, and the things they learned about themselves on the journeys to their finish lines. My hope for non-runners who read this book is that they will be inspired to motion, because motion is what we are designed for.

Not many will have the urge, or time, to go 100 miles on their own two feet. This book is not a challenge to do that. Perhaps few who read this will ever run or walk a 5K, and that, too, is reasonable. But we all need motion for our physical and mental health. Embracing what we are, and finding joy in the process, may be as simple as taking a regular walk down the street. But beware, my first run in the park at age forty-eight took me to the Squamish50/50 finish line.

———

Six weeks after that 50/50, Dad completed his long months of chemo and radiation treatments at the BC Cancer Clinic. By Christmas, the doctors declared he was in remission. Together as a family, we all marvelled at his hair, back thicker than before, along with the surprise reappearance of the locks of curls he had when he was a young man. His brisk walking pace was back to full speed too.

It looks like Dad has a few more miles to go yet. I hope I can keep moving, enduring, and persevering long enough to match him.

Acknowledgements

My first words of thanks go to the runners who spent time with me on the trails over the years, particularly those in Squamish who've been running with me regularly since 2017. You graciously listened to my stories and thoughts about trail running, and time and again you encouraged me to write my stories down to share more widely. Thank you for sharing your insights, and your sometimes outrageous stories that had us all cackling with laughter or flinching in empathetic pain. Thank you for all the joyful trail talks.

Much of this story takes place on the traditional, ancestral, and unceded territory of the Skwxwú7mesh (Squamish) peoples. Those of us who explore its mountains, forests, and valleys are grateful for the opportunity to enjoy, recreate, and share in this beautiful territory.

Six weeks and six-or-so chapters into this writing project, I put a very rough manuscript in the hands of Jen Barsky, fellow runner, scrambler, pacer, and English department head, and asked for her blunt feedback. Jen told me what was working, and more importantly, what wasn't. She was correct in her criticisms and her input gave me the courage to throw at least a third of what was on paper in the trash and rework the entire story arc. What came together after that is a work I'm proud to share. Thank you, friend. You saved this book before it drowned in boring, tedious tables and instruction. Other early readers, Chase Jones and Heather Kennedy, thank you for your encouragement.

First draft readers Laura van der Veer, Cindy Klassen, Solana Green, Alley Vause, Jacquelyn Janzen, Greg Herringer, Jenny

Quilty, John Jones, and Danielle Leroux, thank you for your time and criticisms—each comment made the book better. Steph Corker, the first person to read the full draft, thank you for immediately saying, "Randy, you have to publish this." Krystina Ditson, thanks for your one-day marathon read and direction.

Megan Williams, founder of TSPA The Self Publishing Agency, Inc., thank you for overseeing this project. The team you've assembled to guide new authors, like me, to publication is one of a kind. Thanks also to Ira Vergani, keeper of all schedules and publishing coordinator extraordinaire, and to Anna Mullens, who helped me see the book I actually was writing, not the book I thought I was writing.

Editor Tara McGuire, thank you for your firm-handed guidance, dispassionate notations, humorous comments, and thoughtful inclusions. Editing with you was a master class. Thank you for re-igniting my imagination. My stories became a book under your tutelage.

Book Designer Petya Tsankova, your creativity and artistic vision were a delight. Thank you for being patient with me as I kept tossing ideas your way—knowing your hands were already full.

Elise Volkman and Tage Lee, thanks for your expertise as well.

Special thanks are a must for the co-owners of the Capra Trail & Mountain Running Store in Squamish, BC, Solana Green and Mike Murphy. You created far more than a business when you founded Capra in 2016, you sparked a community. The friendships formed in the footfalls of the Capra fraternity are strong as we move, chase, and endure together.

Jeanette, thanks for running trails and exploring with us, your parents. Your decision to choose the outdoor path for school got Mom and me moving again. Phil, thanks for all our years on the ice. The rink made us better together. Krystie, your moving, chasing, and fleeing are now driven by three little girls—more meaningful than the trails and probably more taxing. Believe it or not, you're already at your next beginning, though it might not feel like that yet.

Most important of all, thanks to Cindy, my bride of forty years, who makes everything better. We're at our best when we're adventuring and wallpapering—go figure. I love how we love to see each other take on new challenges. Let's keep doing that!

Bibliography

DeSalle, Rob, & Tattersall, Ian.
The Brain: Big Bangs, Behaviours, and Beliefs.
New Haven: Yale University Press, 2012; 130.

Gonzales, Laurence.
Deep Survival: Who Lives, Who Dies, and Why.
New York: W. W. Norton & Company, Inc., 2003; 84, 85.

Lavender Smith, Sarah.
The Trail Runner's Companion: A Step-by-Step Guide to Trail Running and racing, from 5Ks to Ultras.
Guilford, CT: Falcon, 2017; 253.

Roberts, David.
Limits of the Known.
New York: W. W. Norton & Company, Inc., 2018; 270, 271, 279.

UltraRunning Magazine.
Volume 40, Issue 5. November 2020; 12-14, 20, 21, 66, 67.

UltraRunning Magazine.
Volume 41, Issue 8. April 2022; 26.

About the Author

Randy Klassen is a dedicated ultrarunner living in Squamish, BC, Canada. A proud father, grandfather, and husband to Cindy for forty years, he is a friend to everyone he meets on the trail. A lifelong storyteller, his happy place is being in a community where people learn, make mistakes, expand personal boundaries, and grow by taking on new challenges.

Manufactured by Amazon.ca
Bolton, ON